Poets and Poetries, Talking Back

COUNTERCLAIMS

POETS AND POETRIES,
TALKING BACK

Edited by H. L. Hix

DALKEY ARCHIVE PRESS
McLean, IL / Dublin

"Introduction," "Overture," "Different," "Attention," "Poetries,"
"Making," "Reimagine," "Left," "Form," "Particularity," "Between,"
"Convergence," "Inexplicable," "Listen," "Prayer," "Necessity," "Time,"
"Refusal," "Citizens," "Ego," "Information," "Memory," "Nuance,"
"Self : World," "Interconnection," and "Coda" copyright © by H. L.
Hix, 2019.

First edition, 2020.

CIP Data: Available upon request.

www.dalkeyarchive.com
McLean, IL / Dublin

Printed on permanent/durable acid-free paper.

Contents

Introduction

IT IS NOT difficult to see, but it is difficult to honor, the distinction between an aspiration and its Aspiration. Honoring the distinction matters, though, because what is lost when the distinction is lost is always the Aspiration. Reduction is reduction to the minuscule. Failing to honor the *distinction*, in other words, confines one to the aspiration. *Counterclaims* seeks to honor the distinction between poetry and Poetry.

Analogy with another domain will help me gesture toward the distinction. In her book *Undoing the Demos*, Wendy Brown argues that neoliberalism, by "transmogrif[ying] every human domain and endeavor, along with humans themselves, according to a specific image of the economic," has become "democracy's conceptual unmooring and substantive disembowelment." As part of her argument, Brown makes in regard to democracy a distinction like the aspiration/Aspiration distinction I am making here in regard to poetry. "'Democracy,'" Brown contends, "signifies the aspiration that the people, and not something else, order and regulate their common life through ruling themselves together." The term "contains nothing beyond the principle that the demos rules"; it "does not specify the arrangements, agreements, or institutions by which popular rule could or should be fulfilled." The principle of rule by the demos, distinct from particular arrangements for enacting that rule, "is the bare promise of bare democracy." The principle "affords without guaranteeing the possibility that power will be wielded on behalf of the many, rather than the few, that all might be regarded as ends, rather

than means, and that all may have a political voice." Honoring
the distinction between the democratic principle and any specific
set of arrangements and institutions made in its name keeps the
principle alive as a critique of the specific arrangements; without
the distinction, the specific *arrangements* are mistaken for democ-
racy, and the principle of rule by the demos is lost.

Translated into my terms, Brown's argument is that neoliber-
alism, by failing to honor the distinction between democracy and
Democracy, loses Democracy altogether. Translated into Brown's
terms, the case made by this book is that a plurivocal poetics
more than a univocal one fulfills the bare promise of bare poetry.

In other words, this project seeks not to take a *position on*, but
to further an ongoing *process of*, poetics. It seeks not to assert a
claim but to perform a heuristic, not to settle on one aesthetic or
one institutional arrangement for poetry, but to fulfill a principle
of continuing dialogue and distributed engagement. By analogy
with Chantal Mouffe's characterization of democracy, this proj-
ect treats poetics as interminably agonistic (a space for claims *and*
counterclaims), and seeks not to "establish a rational consensus"
but to create "collective forms of identification" around poetic
objectives. By analogy with James P. Carse's distinction between
finite and infinite games, this project seeks to extend dialogue
indefinitely, not to agree on who has won but to "bring as many
persons as possible into the play." Or, again, the project seeks
not to prescribe a position, but to operate within a domain, to
take the "responsibility for and toward words" that Václav Havel
contends "is intrinsically ethical."

The project took shape through my posing to various per-
sons (mostly poets and scholars) a question, and gathering the
responses. The question was framed in the following way.

Surely no pronouncements about poetry are cited more fre-
quently than these:

Poetry makes nothing happen. (W. H. Auden, 1939)
To write poetry after Auschwitz is barbaric. (Theodor
Adorno, 1949)

Perhaps each merits repetition: both are plenty provocative, and would move to rumination any reflective person. But the frequency with which they are repeated points to a problem. If sometimes familiarity breeds contempt, sometimes it breeds passive acceptance. Both pronouncements suffer from "the Grecian Urn effect." Keats's closing couplet in that poem ("'Beauty is truth, truth beauty,'—that is all / Ye know on earth, and all ye need to know.") is so catchy and has become so familiar that it carries an aura of authority, as if its truth were self-evident, as if its profundity could be simply taken for granted.

Like the Keats, the Auden and Adorno often are cited as timeless, authoritative truths about poetry, but they were made (as was the Keats) at particular historical moments, in particular cultural contexts, and from particular subject positions. But we (choose any "we" from those of us alive today) occupy various subject positions, live in various circumstances, and stand now nearer the mid-twenty-first century than the mid-twentieth. It is not self-evident that we should (continue to) defer to Auden and Adorno, so "What must or might be said *now* about poetry?"

In the invitation I sent to prospective contributors, posing to each that question, I described a book that "aims to create a dynamic, generative conversation about poetry, by putting each individual contributor into dialogue with her- or himself, with familiar declarations about poetry from Auden and Adorno, and with other contributors to the project." It is the contributors themselves who, with their various, fizzy, sometimes edgy, always insightful responses, have made the book dynamic and generative. I created the structure, the container, for a conversation; they created, with their counterclaims, *the conversation*.

One element of the conversation's structure is manifest in the layout. Except for the "apparatus" (this introduction, the Overture and Coda, the Works Cited), each unit of the project has two main passages, separated by a bullet. Most of the pages begin with the name of the person whose words appear on that page. Above the bullet is a short passage I selected from a previously published work by that contributor: typically from an essay or interview, but always something the person has proposed previously, in a public forum, about poetry. The source of that passage is identified in the "Works Cited" section at the back of the book. Some passages are very recent; others are taken from works written some time ago. Some come from "informal" sources such as interviews and blogs; others come from "formal" sources such as books and scholarly papers. Below the bullet is a new response from the contributor.

A small number of pages have, in bold at the top, not a name but a "regular" word. In those cases, like the others, the first passage is a quotation, and the citation also is given in the "Works Cited" section. Here, though, it is I myself who have provided the second passage, not the person quoted in the first passage. The reader is welcome to receive these interpellations as she or he pleases: as section headings introducing a small cluster of contributions that I associate with one another thematically, or simply as additional entries in the conversation, different in origin from the other entries, but analogous to them in content, similar to them in structure, and continuous with them in sequence.

In "quoting back" to contributors their own prior words, I stuck to a one-hundred-word limit. Regarding the response to be generated, I asked contributors to work within a two-hundred-word limit. The contributor's own prior words thus provided one particular context for her/his new contribution (one claim inviting her/his counterclaim). In addition, those prior words were offered to each prospective contributor as the culmination of a "string" of other contributions to this project. To choose at random just one example, when I solicited a contribution from Tamiko Beyer, I sent her a "string" in which her words were preceded by the prior contributions of David Caplan, Kristin Prevallet, and Rowan Ricardo Phillips. The "string" I had sent Phillips consisted of the prior contributions of Caplan and Prevallet. And so on.

I have positioned two of the contributions as "Interludes,"

on the basis of their scale. Neither was offered in simple defiance of the two-hundred-word frame for contributions; neither was sent me with a request for special dispensation. In one case, the response was sent as a way of *declining* participation, and in the other, the response was sent in order to show me the longer, more complete version of what the contributor had revised into a two-hundred-word reflection. In neither case was the more-than-two-hundred-word response sent with the intention of its being included in the project, but in both cases I asked for and received from the author permission for inclusion.

I assured prospective contributors that "Your response need not be comprehensive, definitive, ultimate. By asking" the same question "of a number of interested parties (poets, scholars, and others), this project seeks not to assemble timeless and authoritative truths able either to ratify or to replace the pronouncements of Auden and Adorno, but to invite and host a provocative, open conversation about poetry." I added by way of rationale that "The project questions the finality and totality of the Auden and Adorno statements, so it could hardly expect finality and totality from any one contribution. Though I hope that the entire conversation will attain a dynamism and profundity, no individual contribution need be "big" or "ultimate" in order to advance the conversation toward that dynamism and profundity."

Each reader of this book is invited to enter into its conversation in her or his own way. One way I myself have tried to do so is by a peculiar form of condensation. I have responded to each passage by each contributor with words of my own, compiling them into an "Overture" and a "Coda." The overture contains responses to the citations of previously published work by the contributors (the passages presented above the bullet on each page), and the coda contains responses to the new words of the contributors (the passages presented below the bullet).

The notes in the overture and coda are not summaries, quite: they do not always concur with, or try to capture, that to which they respond. They do not sum to a manifesto: I myself do not *believe* all that I have included in them. I could hardly: the elements of the overture and the coda do not all concur with one another, any more than the responses of the various contributors concur with one another. They are, to appeal again to Chantal Mouffe's term, agonistic. They do not pretend to integration or wholeness: they may sometimes contradict one another, and they were provoked by the words of others. They *do* try to engage with the conversation that is this book, to reflect on questions it poses, to think through the various insights its contributors offer, to register implications of its contributors' views, to internalize what I take as its truths, to understand why someone else believes what of it I doubt. They try, that is to say, to add yet more counterclaims to this assembly of counterclaims.

A gathering invites (re)arrangement, and the book is itself only one arrangement of the contributions. The invitation process included one arrangement, since I sent prospective contributors "strings" of prior contributions; the blog presentation of the contributions offers another arrangement, the strictly chronological order of their receipt; the book offers one thematically based arrangement. Each arrangement counters the others, and the reader is invited to extend that process, arranging the contributions in mind as he/she wishes.

Counterclaims is no exception to the rule that any sustained and serious attempt to answer one question is sure to raise others. Here are just a few of the questions this project has raised.

Does this book achieve the *opposite* of its intent, solidifying rather than destabilizing what it sets out to interrogate? It purports to question the authority of Auden and Adorno, but does it by its very structure replicate the authorizing they enjoy? The project invites alternatives to the Auden and Adorno, but it does so by asking for alternatives to *them*. Setting up the question in this way may simply grant them from the outset the kind of authority it claims to be testing.

If each entry begins with a previously published statement by the contributor, have I not offered this platform only to persons who already *have* a platform? Have I given voice here only to persons who already have a voice? I have tried not to acquiesce thoughtlessly to "celebrity" measures of poetic credibility (prizes, high-status university affiliations, and so on), since I myself distrust such measures. Persons who enjoy markers of social recognition and prestige are not the only persons capable of wisdom and insight. Still, it may be that in framing the question by quoting previously published work I am ensuring that the book contains only responses from persons "sanctioned" at least to *some* degree.

Is the formulation of the question tendentious, in a way that discriminates against women, persons of color, and others from historically marginalized groups? Early in the process of sending out invitations, I learned that if I wanted the contributions to manifest gender balance, I would have to invite many more women than men. A far higher percentage of men than women responded. Many invitees passively declined (i.e., simply did not respond to the invitation), but of those who actively declined, more than seventy-five percent were women. Similarly disparate response rates held for other identity markers: white invitees compared to invitees of color, and US invitees compared to invitees from other nations. There may be many factors involved, but it has to be asked whether the very conception of the project is flawed in a way that contributes to this discrepancy in response rate.

One contributor identified another question. In her first email reply to me, she notes that "the word limit suggests you are asking for a lot of condensation and aphorism, rather than conversation," and in the email accompanying her contribution, she observes that "there's not a lot of room here for a real conversation." Although I hope that the number and variety of perspectives represented constitutes a real conversation, it is true that the structure of the book invites no one contributor to construct an extended argument.

Another invitee declined to contribute on the grounds that he was simply tired of American poets, who were mostly white, in his view, at least as an attitude if not as a color. This, too, is a critique worth recognizing. Confinement to the English language would be enough by itself to limit the range of the points of view, and the heavy predominance of North American voices limits the range further. The book tries very hard to represent a range of subject positions, but it would be naïve not to observe some of the ways in which the range of subject positions is restricted.

Counterclaims does not *only* raise questions, though; it also proposes various answers. Among the insights its contributors offer, some are singular and others recurring; all are keen. To begin, by noting just a few among the many, a list the reader may extend:

Poetry has affinities with other practices and discursive realms, as Adam Dickinson, for instance, notes when he connects poetry with science on the grounds that "both abductively discern patterns from disparate contexts of knowledge."

Poetry's capacities include that of training the attention, something Elizabeth Macklin captures in her laconic observation that "if poetic practice is anything it's a system of paying attention."

"Poetry" is a singular noun, but what the word denotes might be multiple. Rosebud Ben-Oni, recognizing this, cautions against reduction to singularity: "Beware following a single north star that promises to carry you to poetry, entire."

Poetry can help us address matters of moment and of broad concern, such as race (Phillip B. Williams: "We have to remember what has happened to *all* of our people" (my italics)), class (Gary Lenhart: "we must *invent* a way" to speak of social class (my italics)), and gender (Janice Gould: "Native women's literary maps . . . symbolically provide direction or describe a known, remembered, imagined, or longed-for terrain").

Poetry may be transformative in an intensive sense, the sense Tamiko Beyer identifies when she attributes to poetry the ability to "create shifts inside our bodies and in our minds," or in an extensive sense, as Ajuan Maria Mance recalls to mind by citing "what the poet Audre Lorde once called a shift in the 'quality of light by which we scrutinize our lives.'"

Early in his book *Cosmodernism*, Christian Moraru identifies as one of its organizing premises the conviction that the "self-edifying moment occurs not as self and other 'iron out' their differences nor as these discrepancies and asymmetries prove superficial and our 'common humanity' triumphantly shines through them, but precisely by means of such dissonances, due to them rather than despite them." *Counterclaims* shares that premise. It seeks to occasion the self-edifying moment not by repressing differences, or by declaring victory for one position over others, or by pretending some universality, but *through* rather than *despite* differences.

In *The Necessary Angel*, Wallace Stevens laments an artistic degeneracy caused by a "failure in the relation between the imagination and reality" that he attributes to "the pressure of reality," which he describes as "the pressure of an external event or events on the consciousness to the exclusion of any power of contemplation." Bonnie Costello employs Stevens's term in order to make a point not about the degeneracy of art but about the vigor of poetry. Costello questions the usual dichotomy between poetry in its "traditional commitment to the individual" and poetry that is "focused instead on collective experiences," by noting one way in which they harmonize. Poetry, she says, "may be most needed in its traditional function when the effect of great public upheaval is to undermine or destroy the feeling for individual life." In such cases, according to Costello, "the role of poetry becomes to reawaken the sense of one's own life, not as an alternative to the world but as a 'radiant and productive atmosphere' in which to confront that great pressure of reality."

Costello's words were written before *Counterclaims* had even begun, but they perfectly characterize its orienting ambition to enact a principle of inclusive and agonistic dialogue rather than valorizing a position or fixing a point of view, and to confront the pressure of reality by reflecting on poetry in a way that, in her words, "precedes any political determination, though it may indeed refresh one's life as a citizen."

Overture

Meaning means form. Form forms meaning.

To secure beauty and truth, practice insecurity.

The poem pledges the self to the other-than-self.

No self sees itself except by seeing itself as other-than-self.

A poem's closest sisters need not be other poems.

Affinities between poems propose affinities between persons.

Dismissing any poem discloses not *its* failure but *mine*.

Poetry *for* all the people, poetry *of* all the people.

Scale-scrambler ensmalls the large and enlarges the small.

Violence, virus. Violent language, host.

It takes practice, it would *be* a practice, to resist *what* one should, *when* one should, *as* one should, and *because* one should.

Far from establishing *stasis*, metaphor detonates *dynamis*.

One metaphor to tend the hearth; one, the fields.

Compose the inexplicable, explain the incomposite.

Feed illocution, starve perlocution.

She sang against the last violence, to denounce the next.

Recognize the *magnitude* of otherness in its *multiplicity*.

Concentricity I: poetry within society within nature. Concentricity II: nature within society within poetry.

One world, given and made.

First person in poetry. *So the last shall be first, and the first last.*

What I hear : how I sing.

Awakened from dream into dreamt.

Poetry a type of elegy, not vice versa.

Art and life, as separate as sign and referent, and as intertwined.

Born *of* the absence it is born *into*, poetry fills the absence it is full of.

Not itself revelation, poetry nonetheless sings what revelation reveals.

Right rhythm, right words.

Motherless and fatherless, itself neither mother nor father, the made remakes gender.

Process, as claimed, but still product, condemned to commodification.

Poetry cannot defeat relentless monetization, but can defy it, can stand, grocery bags in hand, before its line of tanks.

Only what belongs to no one belongs to all.

To delight, to teach: poetry need do neither. Align oneself with the world thus, yes, but also otherwise.

I thought I knew. I should have known better.

If self-knowledge were *given*, I would not need *means* for showing myself to myself, for recognizing myself in the world.

"Poetry" names one particular means for sorting out identity, and also names *everything* one does in the sorting out.

Variety and breadth are not identical, but poetry works to correlate them.

Until we name past trauma, we are powerless to prevent future trauma. Still, we ought not mistake the naming for the prevention.

As if my verbal self could partition itself from my material self.

Poem, person: equally in and of the body.

Forced back into my body, though I never left it.

Trapped in this my body, I am equally astonished that nothing else is, and that I myself am.

The poem a map to be followed, but a map *of* what, *to* where?

I hear you whenn I hear your words. I hear your words whenn I hear you.

Against subjection, dialogue.

Poetic deconstruction, because in replacing one binary with
another it's the replacing, not the new binary, that matters.

To test the un- in unimaginable.

We may, and should, reason toward conscience. And *imagine*
toward conscience.

The scope of the failure of contemporary public imagination is
unimaginable.

Proximity a metaphor for poetic imperatives: look closely,
listen closely.

Does its being more articulate than a moan make poetry more
effective? More beautiful? More true?

Math one measure, poetry another.

Poetic math: one person, two; one person, all.

Original because unrepeatable. Expressive because unrepeat-
able. Disclosive because unrepeatable.

An ocean separates art from life, but still their shorelines match.

One poem isolates my losses, another matches them to the
sounds that disturb my sleep.

Whoever thought "aesthetic" a fit category for poetry?

I bent my language to the world, and called the bending po-
etry. I bent my world to the language, and called the bending
poetry. Now I bend myself to the language, and still have no
better name for the bending.

Poetry, because even the immediate defies non-contradiction.

Of continental drift all I can feel is the occasional quaking.

Grandiosities be damned. Poetry, the most makeshift of make-shift responses to makeshift circumstances.

Makers of culture make culture *of* culture: they make what they make because they've been given what they've been given.

Like a language, a culture lives by, or dies for lack of, transla-tion.

I'll show you my cultural archive if you'll show me yours.

False dilemma, that a poem occupy the interior of an individ-ual or of a culture.

Thought as fast as the thinking is slow.

By distributing unevenly the imperative to modesty, we dis-tribute unjustly the right and the means of *address*.

No thinking without dualisms, but we can think *with* dual-isms *away from* dualisms rather than toward them.

Epic the map of the wanderings, lyric the wanderer's arrest warrant.

If epic occurs in the domain of assembly and debate, lyric takes place in the contested space between concealment and disclosure.

The quietest poem shouts down the loudest self-assertion.

Rebut one silence with another.

Surrounded by shouting, share a whisper.

To speak out I might take up my pen, or I might set it down.

When the poem comes to life, *I* come to life.

Poetry *between* the real and the ideal, and *as the merger of* real and ideal.

Lab experiment. Thought experiment. Word experiment.

The experiment we call a poem has, and wants, no control.

To change and *keep changing* what I see, how I see, with whom I speak, to whom I listen, how I secure silence within and despite the torrent.

What we see matters less than what we see by.

Change perception, change perceived. Turn away from offered sights, see what you have been forbidden to see.

Than poetry, no speculation better replicates the etymological sense of "speculation."

Collect yourself. Gather your thoughts. How infrequently we note that those imperatives apply not intermittently but always.

Because freaks of nature are fully as natural as anything else.

What are the implications of my being implicated?

Poetry the substitute for better understanding of what better understanding would entail.

Poetry need not *advance* me toward the vision, to *turn* me toward it.

God didn't value the Tower of Babel, but nothing compels us to concur in that judgment.

Poetry, itself a technology, infiltrates each new communication technology it encounters.

With some technologies (scales, say) in some contexts (grocery store, post office) we want units constant. With poetry, best to keep recalibrating.

In the age of digital reproduction, in which my text or image can be instantly and infinitely reiterated, older forms of copying take on new force. Reinscription—rewriting a document by hand—becomes an act of resistance, memorization an act of defiance.

Before it became a tool of corporate data collection, intertextuality was an instrument of song.

They also swerve who don't command much freight.

The crisis interpreted to me the clues that would have helped me avert the crisis, had I understood them sooner.

Had it tributaries, this inland sea might host more life.

If anything *could* make me more human, poetry would.

No ideal more absurd and impossible than "self-definition."

Lost poetry, lost poetics. And vice versa.

The poetic killjoy, sibling to the feminist killjoy.

To invent a vocabulary adequate to the unspeakable.

To hear not the speaker but the spoken to.

I could call this movement a migration if it held hope of return.

Brick laments as ruin what weeds relish as restoration.

Irreducible, because attentive to irreducibility.

Alive, because alive *to*.

No one owns the language, but anyone willing to homestead in it can find a place.

Divinize humanity, to humanize divinity.

Sense like a beast, think like a god.

Poetry envisages revolutions, large and small, public and private.

The inner world and the outer. Only what inhabits neither can see both.

Because the established order is established by keeping what establishes it silent and invisible, poetry—*any* non-standard language use—ever defies the established order. Or (the same thing) establishes another order.

Not everything in my poetry originates outside myself. Yet.

Bury radioactive waste, and it leeches into the soil and the groundwater. Same with poetry.

Strange hostility attractor.

What poems are good at tells more about the good than the good tells about what poems are good at.

The market, *increase*. Poetry, *care*.

Featherless, but not voiceless. I cannot fly, but I can sing.

I am not yet music, but I have not stopped trying to be.

The inhuman, the inhumane: each an absence, a want, of poetry.

Someone has to worry the proximity between the wrong and the wronged.

Testify to one wrong, resist another.

What to do with my degree from the college of inconsequence?

The layered temporalities that imbue God with eternity only perforate the poem with contingency.

To make the present most intensely present, should I look toward the future or the past?

The one who critiques Our Way is not one of Us.

If it echoes around the canyon, is it still one cry from one bird?

That's what we rewrite when we rewrite: not our poems but ourselves and the codes against which we ought to chafe.

Not in the name of history but in the face of history.

As in horse training, addressing something directly may not be the most intimate approach.

Poem, poetry. Replacing our nouns with verbs (let us poem today, I poem you) would emphasize that poetry is not so much *contained* in an *artifact* as it is *enacted* in an *encounter*.

What I see and what I hear might not harmonize automatically. They might need a third note, what I say or what is said to me, to become a chord.

Of sensibilities, the most pluralized and pluralizing is the most singular.

Extension of who I listen to enlarges what I hear.

Any self-renewal would be curtailed by my mortality, but I *can* participate in renewal of the language.

Art develops what it develops from.

Performs no accounting, submits to none.

War *can be* perpetual because it *is* futile. Try as I might, I can neither extend my claim on you, nor erase your claim on me.

Language does enough excluding, without our inviting national alliances to do more.

Let us now praise porous borders.

I made these promises because I believed those lies.

Which poetic affiliations are igneous, which sedimentary, which metamorphic?

Resisting injustice proves harder than we thought, beyond the reach of our goodwill. Still, how learn to resist, if not from poetry?

The nothing that is not aware, and the nothing that is.

We do not face nature after the manner of facing another human. I look "out" from within non-you me, across a gap to non-me you. But there is no non-nature me out of whom to look, and no gap across which to look. Romantic poetry helped us construct our current understanding of humans in nature. We need poetry's help again, to revise that understanding.

The faults in speech speak, too, not only the perfections.

Better uncompromised than uncompromising.

The capacity to stipulate, and the capaciousness to absorb stipulation.

Story, mystery from above; poem, from within.

Observational distance, emotional proximity.

The voice. The voice. The voice. The voice. The voice.

Never layers enough. Think what the thought of one thinking about thought would think.

So immersed are we in instrumentality that making nothing happen is the only form opposition can take.

The water is wide, to make crossing it a transformation.

What I cannot comprehend, give me to constellate.

I cling to what is slipping away, *not* so that it will not slip away, but so that I *will*.

Counterclaims

POETS AND POETRIES,
TALKING BACK

Different

"YOU MUST CHANGE your life!"—this is the imperative that exceeds the options of hypothetical and categorical. It is the absolute imperative—the quintessential metanoetic command . . . The numinous authority of form enjoys the prerogative of being able to tell me "You must." It is the authority of a different life in this life.

*

We urge transformation on ourselves (*I'm going to lose twenty pounds this year!*) and on one another (*Repent!*). The urging might be accompanied by example (*Arnie from Accounting took off ten and he looks great*) or by instruction (*Chew with your mouth closed*).

Poetry offers instead a field in which transformation becomes intelligible: a metamorphic imaginary, a landscape of renewal. The new self enters the world first in and as imagination. The new self is made by making.

Meena Alexander

WHY DO WE have poetry in a time like this? For me that question folds into another: What does it mean to belong in a violent world? I think of the invisible archive that each of us bears within, a deeply personal ingathering of sights and sounds and scents and bits of the sometimes ruined materiality that memory allots—and perhaps this is another way of thinking about the coruscating flow of the inner life that gives meaning to our existence, all that comes up when we dare to say "I." And surely this is the province of poetry.

*

Yes the unspeakable is with us, but all the more reason for the poem to exist. The poem is like light that alters nothing but changes everything. Now I think that poetry allows us to slip into another self, the soul-self if you wish that is seamlessly bound to the sensorial power of the body and yet is unerringly marked by the ineffable. To make poems now, in our new century, is to know that words can only go so far, that they are etched on a silence that composes us, even as we jostle and shift and turn in the wild whirring world. Who am I? Who are we? In answer to these impossible questions, poetry brings us face to face with the mystery of being, the dark mirror of language, polished, gleaming.

Robin Becker

IN POEMS, TIME may contract or expand; forgotten memories may rise up to form iconic images. The art of poetry allows us to fly as well as walk, to be old and young at once, to be inside and outside personal experience. And in poetry we may combine the real and the ideal, the concrete and the abstract.

*

What "happens" when we write or read poems changes our inner lives—slowly or powerfully or lightly, or glancingly or forever-ly. Sometimes, the effort to understand another's way of putting together a sentence suffices. Sometimes, a startling juxtaposition of images arrests our vision. Almost never does "nothing" change for me, even when I find myself resisting a cluster of words. That resistance itself creates some nodule of meaning that works like grit to annoy or nudge another change along. As a Jew, I understand Adorno's claim. Historically located, his statement seeks to extinguish a world that would extinguish him. We go on from there.

Jan Conn

EXPERIMENTAL DESIGN IN science is often very creative, and novel insights that lead to the resolution of complex scientific problems are sometimes discovered when the conscious mind, full of relevant, detailed information, is allowed to drift or rest and subconscious images or even formulae surface. Since the beginnings of oral poetic tradition, dreams, both nighttime and daytime, have been fertile ground. Inside the overlap resides concise use of language to communicate information as clearly as possible . . .

*

The quotes by Auden and Adorno have always struck me as very Eurocentric and far from my own world experience. Naively, I refused to be at the mercy of what I perceived as European historical opinion, perhaps from being brought up in a small mining town in southeastern Quebec, or having spent much of my adult life focused on poetry or in Latin America exploring some aspect of public health, malaria, and mosquitoes. Poetry might occasionally appear barbaric, but it is a form of survival, essential to some. I want poetry that shakes me awake. For me, certain talismanic poems stimulate a reaction or a series of them, albeit interiorly, as though I had chanced upon a doorknob. Poetry can "shatter fixed ideas" as Mary Ruefle notes. Yes, even scientific ideas. Which often fail to be concise or communicative. Possibly because they are not, to quote Rilke, "Exposed on the cliffs of the heart." The artist Susan Dimitman took a series of powerful, absorbing photographs of graffiti in Portland. In one, inside thick strips of smeared black paint someone scratched the letters I M. In Memoriam or stark affirmation of being? Both are poetry, or neither is.

Lisa D. Chávez

[W]HAT I LOVE best about story is that moment when I am gone, when I'm wholly in the head of the character, whether that be a character in a three-hundred-page novel or in a two-page poem. I want to be transported . . . That is what story does. It is both truth and fiction, and it lets us live other lives. And when we write narrative poetry, we are drawing on one of the oldest human traditions, the telling of tales that transform.

*

Our poems exist, like us, in the Now, but with the power of imagination we can escape the shackles of time, existing both here and in the past or future: re-seeing one, imagining another. Poetry's magic: to look forward and back, and to not be trapped by the tyranny of what is, but to transform with words. Poetry can bear witness, and the simple act of recording injustice in words can change it, because poetry is the voice that says "someone sees." Poetry is more relevant now than ever as it records our disparate experiences, sings some of our fragmented experiences whole. Whether political or not, a poem, for a moment, shares the writer's sense of the world, and that is powerful indeed. A poem may not stop bullets or wars, but what it might do is change a reader's perceptions, and in that change—however small—lay the seeds of something that may grow into action, and that action might bring change. Whether it is a call to political action that motivates a reader to join a cause, or an observation of beauty that leaves a reader calmer, kinder, even incremental shifts in perception can change the future.

Changming Yuan

[I]N TERMS OF traditional Chinese poetics, a fine poem ought to contain a "poetic eye," that is, something really fresh, witty, sensual, intriguing, soul-enriching or imagination-stimulating. As Badiou has strongly suggested, it would be imperative for the poet to say either something relatively new in a well-accepted way or something already existent in a relatively new way. Since the reader, targeted or not, plays an important role in this aspect, the poet becomes deeply involved in cultural politics with or without intention; indeed, the claim of no political stance or interest is itself a political manifesto.

*

It is true that even if poets are to become legislators in contemporary democracies, or government officials as in ancient China, their poetic works can hardly create any social impact; it is also true that today's poetry is being driven into a corner by all kinds of e-devices besides the entertaining industry; however, poetry will never die, insofar as humans are still interested in ideas, language and beauty. For me, every poem is a micro artistic system of semiotic symbols used for human communication. This being so, poetry has not only given us much reading pleasure, but will also help us more to enhance our spiritual wellness. Poetry may have made nothing happen in Auden's (outer) world, but is making everything happen in our inner worlds. History will show its social effect on the human mind as it becomes deformed and degraded in a derailed age.

Tamiko Beyer

To BE QUEER is to be a freak of nature. To write about *nature* as a queer, then, is to begin by questioning of all previous assumptions of what *nature* is. To write in the queer::eco::poetics realm is to begin by interrogating the construction of what is *natural*, and all of what *natural* implies (inevitable, innate, normal, non-human, pristine, etc.).

The double colon of queer::eco::poetics breathes new life into co-opted, saturated forms, wrestling both queerness and green-washing away from corporate /mainstream speech acts.

*

We—all of us :: human, animal, stone, plant :: existing now—are hurtling toward a destruction created by humans actions in the Global North, driven by capitalism run rampant. This is truer now than it was four years ago.

In the US today, deep racial injustices are seemingly more visible to more people than four years ago, and more people are outraged and organizing.

Every day, poetry wakes me in the form of the river sounds outside my window. Poems by Adrienne Rich and Joy Harjo hanging above my desk keep me moving through hectic days challenging transnational corporations. And I fall asleep in the poem of my body intertwined with my girlfriend's. Poetry has always been synonymous with the world's deep mystery.

Poetry cannot stop the destruction we are causing. But we—humans—can, or at least we can change the ways we treat the world and all that exists in it, and so, perhaps, slow or stem the destruction. Poetry can create shifts inside our bodies and in our minds—those fish—in ways that we will never understand. If we (all of us) are to survive, those shifts must happen. Poetry just might help us get there.

Sawnie Morris

"In this way / could she" begins Valerie Martínez's book-length lyric poem concerning the murder of hundreds of girls and women over the past two and half decades, many of them employed by US owned maquiladoras (factories) on the Mexican side of the US–Mexican border . . . As is the case with many postmodern poems of resistance, we trust *Each and Her* in part because the speaker implicates and interrogates her own position while examining the socio-economic and cultural forces that have made the murders and their growing numbers possible.

*

All poems worth their salt rise from the unconscious and place their maker at risk. The poet calls on imagination with the shamanic aspects of poetry's rhythms and arranging impulses, to— as Martinez states in the final fragment "—remake the world." Martinez's poems form a life-altering ceremony in the same way that the *Hymn to Inanna*, inscribed four thousand years ago in what is now southern Iraq, is a ceremony—or, in the way that Brenda Hillman's honoring of the four elements, or Mark Nowak's *Shut Up Shut Down*, or Claudia Rankine's *Citizen*, or Anne Waldman's *Manatee/Humanity* are all life-altering ceremonies; in their subtlest tracings and patterns, these poems "make something happen." Perhaps the something that happens is "merely" an interior liberation for the poet/reader, but I doubt it. The symbiotic nature of existence coupled with quantum physics makes an impact across time/place far more likely. To *not* have written poetry after Auschwitz would mean being stuck at a particular coordinate in the confines of chronology, frozen in a hell-bardo. Earth-centered cultures have always recognized poetry's ability to alter the world. It is maker and made. It is mother and mystery and matrix; it is the *yes, you may.*

Suzanne Gardinier

OUR SHARED LANGUAGE in this place and time is heavy with lies, bled and distorted, words of greeting and blessing and parting spoken by machines or hollowed into the shilling between seller and sold; it also brims and burns with insistent unruly hybrid life. It is from this *mestizaje* that the new commonwealth, a world that will hold all the people, if there is to be one, will come . . . [T]he new commonwealth must be made first with visions, in the way we know how to share them: with words.

*

Re **n o w** & a poet's work : "taking part in an immense shift in human consciousness" (Adrienne Rich)
      (For someone whose first poetry reading was by Adrienne Rich & Audre Lorde in 1979, Auden's "poetry makes nothing happen" sounds like a message from when humans thought the sun revolved around the earth.)

Rich quoting Gramsci: "One must speak of a struggle for a new culture, that is, for a new moral life that cannot but be intimately connected to a new intuition of life, until it becomes a new way of feeling and seeing reality and, therefore, a world intimately ingrained in 'possible artists' and 'possible works of art.'"

Edward Said to Mahmoud Darwish in Darwish's poem: "If I die before you, my will is the impossible."

Judith Butler: "So how, then, might we understand the impossible—is it precisely the life that is not defined by death, but by some horizon of life?"

Adorno, "On Lyric Poetry & Society": ". . . we are not concerned with the poet as a private person, not with his [sic] psychology or so-called social perspective, but with the poem as a philosophical sundial telling the time of history."

René Char: "We must write poems, but we must not stop there."

Attention

FREEDOM IS NOT strictly the exercise of will, but rather the experience of accurate vision which, when this becomes appropriate, occasions action. It is what lies behind and in between actions and prompts them that is important, and it is this area which should be purified. By the time the moment of choice has arrived the quality of attention has probably determined the nature of the act.

*

In the contemporary market-dominated mindset, it is easy to view freedom as absence of regulation (as in "free market" and "free trade"). But it is possible to regard freedom in other terms. If to be free is only to be allowed to increase, without impediment or limit, the quantity of capital I control, then poetry has no bearing on freedom. If, though, my freedom has to do not with the size of my bank account but with the quality of my attention, poetry is not irrelevant but necessary.

Cynthia Hogue

THE FAILURE TO possess the woman of the West's poetic legends is often the occasion for a poem's coming into existence. Displaying herself in some way, on a walk or with her flock, the woman invites notice (in essence, asks for it) . . . The violent appropriation of the feminine figure by the masculine that so often comprises in poetic convention the enunciatory moment—rape sublimated as poetic ravishing—illuminates the ideological specificity of sexual difference and its relation historically to poetry and aesthetic representation.

*

I have in the last several years been thinking about writing as translating / trans*form*ing emotional material, in the sense that a poem "translates" something observed or experienced, the pure emotion of it, into material form: by writing, we are *translating* lived experience, embodied emotions, into another medium. Suddenly there is a transformation or a transmutation. *Translating* is an act (or as an act) of "witnessing," actually, of "bearing witness" (to that which is invisible, physiological or unconscious). The writing translates *embodied emotional knowledge* into art. It requires the actions of both poiesis and translation (translation as conveying something in one form or language into another form or language). To forge an aesthetic composition out of strong emotion is to bring an *attentiveness* to the process of feeling feelings that transforms, transmutes, transmits and transfers the feelings into something that bears witness to their passage but IS not itself emotional because the emotional material is speechless, wordless, but embodied, held in and by our bodies and therefore accessible.

David Borthwick

ECOPOETRY IS A subtle form of activism. Poetry is . . . one of the few forms it is difficult to make conform to corporate utility, its fundamental features acknowledging complexity and the difficulty of expression, rather than endorsing simplicity, instant apprehension, the superficially clear yet disposable sound-bite. Poetry's notorious instability of meaning, its protean shifting, its rhythmic soundings, resist swift dismissal. Poetry is a terrestrial channel in a digital age, grounded and grounding, set firmly in the soil of the real.

*

What tickled me about the word "terrestrial" was its Latin etymology in "earth". The Scottish poet Kathleen Jamie talks in "The Tree House" about "our difficult / chthonic anchorage" and it's this sense of "grounding" I had in mind. Poetry is particularly adept at interrogating the difficulty of anchorage on the earth, I feel, perhaps because it need not be confined (unless it wants to be) by some of the constraints of other genres (the anthropo-centric need for dramatic event or plot, for example). At a time when the novel remains the preeminent literary form for docu-menting "our times", it seems to me that poetry is really where the action is. The contemporary eco-poetry movement is richly diverse in its experimentation and commitment—a literary form often treated outside academe as marginal in some senses is at the very heart of negotiating pressing, difficult questions. We must always find means to do so.

As to poetry's inherent instability, I stand by this as an inherent strength, a means of capturing while evading capture. The late Martin Harrison once wrote about an ecological work as one whose form was "undetermined" or "not fully resolved", which performed "an evolving act of attention or attentiveness." His words ring true.

Shabnam Piryaei

GOOD POETRY, LIKE all good art, reflects our complexity, our ambiguity; this gesturing toward countless truths is part of what makes art so very valuable. Demanding immediate and clear-cut answers of it reduces it, in the same way that demanding a person to be only one thing reduces and misrepresents them.

*

Poetry, like any creative act, can serve as a rupture to the violences enacted by the many closures we impose, demand, submit to, and reinforce. In particular the violence of knowledge-as-containment, of knowledge-as-possession; and the violence of absolute and singular answers, of an absolute and singular understanding, which ultimately sever one's responsibility toward the other. As Audre Lorde writes, "There is no separate survival." And in order to confront our never-ending responsibilities toward one another's survival, one must enact and endure sustained scrutiny—of ourselves, our habits, our traditions, our institutions, our relationships, our power. The verbal sparseness of the medium of poetry, and the tremendous focus and weight involved, for me, in the construction and placement of every word, summons the necessity of scrutiny as a way of being. This critical examination is bound to intimacy, and to the patience and strength required for one to inhabit the fertile discomfort of such closeness, such lingering and disclosure.

Elizabeth Macklin

EVERY POET SOMEHOW learns to deal with the "outer ear" of the hostile reader, and its insistent, accompanying inner voice. For poets who are women, the voice of the hostile reader is perhaps oftenest male, although of course not necessarily. The terror in swerving—breaking out and inward, saying the needful next thing—is that of going over the edge . . .

*

I still believe there's a difference between swerving into the matter of a poem and veering off, and away, from it. Though now I think I was wrong—perhaps—given the haste the two words imply. Because if poetic practice is anything it's a system of paying attention: attention in Simone Weil's sense of the word. *Attention* as opposed to the quick exertion of *Will*. A way of using judgment, or (per Carson) the sense of smell—a reverse poetic license, anyhow, since attention allows the individual human poet a final swerve, so as not to veer away from reality.

Since that essay was published, the "outer ear" has in this country and elsewhere become more insistent in its hostility. I continue to think of the first time I ever heard a voice lowered to speak about politics in the United States, suddenly in a near whisper; it happened within a dozen days of September 11, 2001.

For part of what I need to say about the Adorno, see the last section of Deborah Eisenberg's essay on the (formerly East)

German novelist Jenny Erpenbeck's latest work in the 4/2/2015 *New York Review of Books*, where it's discussed.

Regarding the Auden: "Nothing"?

Valerie Martínez

[POETRY IS] A different kind of language. It's not the language of direction, it's the language of indirection. We have plenty of language in our culture that gets at things directly. Poetry preserves a place in language where you can meander, where you can be circular, where you can get at things in a different way.

Poetry forces you to stop. It slows you down . . . To have someone spend fifteen minutes on four lines, that's a really beautiful thing. That means somebody is honoring language.

*

". . . nothing less than the most radical imagination will carry us beyond this place . . ."

Adrienne Rich, *On Lies, Secrets, and Silence: Selected Prose, 1966–1978*, quoted in *Each and Her* by Valerie Martínez (Univ. of Arizona Press, 2010). Epigraph.

Adrienne Rich, on receiving the 2006 Medal for Distinguished Contribution to American Letters, reminded us that "the accusation famously invoked in Adorno ('after the Holocaust lyric poetry is impossible') he later retracted and a succession of Jewish poets have in their practice rejected." Later in this speech Rich said: "Poetry has the capacity in its own ways and by its own means to remind us of something we are forbidden to see, a forgotten future, a still uncreated site whose moral architecture is founded not on ownership and dispossession, torture and bribes, outcast and tribe, but on the continuous redefining of freedom."

What I want to say about poetry *now* is more about readers—all of us who write (I hope) and those who deeply read, dip into, encounter, or someday may encounter poetry. The reason we should be seriously engaged in promoting the reading of poetry as a practice at the heart of community life is precisely because of its power to invoke (among other things) "still uncreated sites," "architecture founded not on ownership and dispossession," and redefinitions of freedom. Crucial corollaries are the pause, concentration and reflection—perhaps even changes in action—that reading poetry asks of us in a culture that pushes us away from the singular, sustained, contemplative moment.

Lee Ann Roripaugh

[P]ERHAPS EVERY POEM is a mirror box of sorts. Imagine our mirror neurons, lit up and flickering like glittery circuit boards, in mirrored response to every poem that we read. Indeed, the implications of mirror neurons, with respect to the ways in which we think about how we read and make poems, seems profound. Perhaps a poem teaches the brain, through language, things that are beyond the body's comprehension. Perhaps—at least on the neurocognitive level—poetry really does make things happen, after all.

*

I can't help but feel that conversations about the utility and/or barbarity of poetry have served their purpose—curdling into their own types of master narratives that, at their worst, generate an aesthetic response of self-consciousness to the point of preciousness, and/or helpless passivity. Having acknowledged the problems of language (its embedded systemic hegemonies, its failures to (re)present, its enmeshment and complicity with institutionalized machines), perhaps it now becomes important to ask what language, what poetry, *can* do. Neurocognitively speaking a lot, I would suggest: challenge a reader's perceptions, assumptions, modes of thinking, preconceived histories, and ideologies; foster attentiveness (to language, to others, to the surrounding world); create new neural pathways in the brain in lieu of neural ruts developed in response to sociocultural clichés and as coping mechanisms to trauma; create a collaborative empathic exchange between poet and reader (exchange of intellect, exchange of information/knowledge, exchange of aesthetic style, exchange of sensory perception, exchange of emotion). Language is action. It's the medium by which we act upon the world, and through which the world is enacted upon us, and it's perhaps through its comparative lack of capitalist utility, or even interpersonal agenda, that the poem becomes the purest possible form of this enactment.

Susan Wheeler

[ALTHOUGH] THE TASK of *registering poems* (take it, perhaps, as the proactive alternative to *being branded*) in the culture is indeed Herculean, it is not by fault of this ambition. The ambition to find language combinations, structures, methods of composition, that remain *unassimilable* in the broad banality of the cultural market should not be faulted, should not be construed as "digging our own hole."

*

Where are we, now, in this culture? Jumpy, over-vigilant, alert for incoming missives or missiles, overfed, under-challenged, exhausted by work, overwhelmed by information, isolate, quick to escape, to zone out, to get high, to obsess, to log on. Poets who strive not to reify where we are but to open a porthole to another way of focusing, of being, of thinking, serve a *resistance* utopian and essential.

Poetries

THE GREAT DANGER is single-mindedness: reducing things to one perspective, one idea, one overriding rule.

*

A noun can function to pick out the membership of a set with clear and definite boundaries established by a single principle, as with "carnivore." What eats meat is a carnivore, what does not is not. But as Wittgenstein observes, a noun can also—instead—register a cluster of family resemblances, as with "game." What baseball and bingo share in common need not match what poker and parcheesi share. There is reason to think that, in this regard, "poetry" behaves more like "game" than like "carnivore."

David Caplan

INSTEAD OF ASSIGNING stable values to poetic forms, we need the patience to trace the forms' shifting movements, as their political and their aesthetic uses accommodate new imperatives and contexts. We must attend to the complications that make poetic forms fascinating . . . [Poetic form has the] ability to claim contradictory political meanings. Because verse form is essentially senseless—an iamb, for instance, merely defines an abstract pattern—it stays open to multifold meanings, to new uses and unexpected inflections.

*

"The words of a dead man /Are modified in the guts of the living," Auden observes earlier in the poem that Hix quotes as one of our discussion's source texts. No truths about poetry are eternal. Just as the art is always changing, individual poems transform language and are transformed. They frustrate the desire to arrive at conclusions, to "nail down" a particular meaning or idea. Auden's elegy dramatizes this point. Five lines after he offers the canonical statement, "Poetry makes nothing happen," Auden modifies it, calling poetry "A way of happening, a mouth." Perhaps the best way to understand poetry—to read it with full appreciation, pleasure, and the appropriate skepticism—is to remain alert to how it modifies its own positions, as well as ours. To live with poetry is to hear the same words differently, to hear poetries, not poetry, "A way of happening, a mouth."

Kristin Prevallet

THE LACK OF communication between the living and the dead makes the living wild with fear. It is in this distance, the space between, that grieving finds form in poetry. This form scatters its content into sometimes incommunicable terrain, diffusing meaning (splatter) as if trying to connect the multitude of suffering. Being open to receive this splatter of meaning hesitantly transmitted through difficult language is one way to practice living with uncertainty and doubt.

*

I love David Caplan's sentence: "Because verse form is essentially senseless—an iamb, for instance, merely defines an abstract pattern—it stays open to multifold meanings, to new uses and unexpected inflections." This is what I call "splatter"—how poetic forms aren't pre-fixed, they're evolving. Lately I have been thinking about how poetries capture language anomalies whose characteristic feature is their stubborn refusal to be assimilated into existing paradigms. Forms (and, I think structures of any kind, including buildings, no matter how comprehensive and seemingly stable) are parameters around a field that allows the field to find form. They evolve and possibly they disintegrate as new structures and new fields find form, and so on, into the infinity that is language. So in the field of language poets are the labyrinth and the walls; the anxiety and the love; the atrocity and the healing. Poetries are simultaneity.

Forrest Gander

IF THE LANGUAGE practices commandeering world history are increasingly standardized, utilitarian, and transcriptional, poetry offers a different order of relationship with the other.

*

Must be said? The "musts," the apodeictic assertions, the righteousness, the surety, the commands, the assumptions, the bullying stances of the imperative; aren't we through with them? The forty-three kidnapped Mexican students *must* be brought home safely; that was the first demand. What did "must" mean in that context? *Might be said?* Now as ever, anything. Poetry is the blue Andalusian rooster swallowing pebbles in a New Orleans cemetery and it is this very sentence revised into a context-free grammar plus a rhinoplasty. Poetry's name is legion, and still, by some simplifying, metaphoric, wholesale luck, we sometimes encounter thought and feeling and flashes of intuition choiring in an arrangement of words. Many avert their face. I cannot take my distance from it. *Might be felt?* Everything. Since poetry has such a high degree of informational entropy, the richness of messages carried on its particular channels is incalculable. Human experience, what might be thought and sensed, may be modeled more by poetry than by any other language activity. Until we acknowledge that richness, the multiplicity in ourselves, how can we begin to develop the self into the fullness of its selfness?

Craig Dworkin

[T]HE UMBRELLA TERM "poetry" may not be very useful. Worse yet, it may well lead to the kind of confusions Ludwig Wittgenstein termed "grammatical errors." Because we have a single term, we imagine that all of the things designated by that term share a family resemblance. The category of "poetry" inclines us to forget that one "poem" may have much more to do with a film, or a musical composition, or something else entirely than with another text that also happens to be called a poem.

*

The umbrella term "poetry" may still not be very useful. Poetry has been such a generous host over the last quarter century that its capaciousness would seem to have no bounds. From the prose of the new narrativity to the transcriptions of conceptual writing, texts that might otherwise have been considered "experimental fiction" or "essays" or "contemporary art" have found a comfortable home, or at least temporary refuge, under the sign of "poetry." We should be grateful guests, but as the purview of that aegis expands, the urgency of specifying what exactly one means by it in any particular context increases proportionally.

The term often seems to indicate a hazy sense of approval ("poetry" is the name we give to texts we like) rather than anything specifically descriptive (such as the Slavic Formalists' definition of "language oriented away from the communicative function")—*poetry* is the master term in a language of value.

Accordingly, the same evaluative function has seeped into sub-genres as well, as if "avant-garde" or "conceptual" were a badge of honor (forgetting Hugh Kenner's admonition that "the avant-garde can be just as boring as anything else"). A language of precision, rather than vague praise, would serve poetics well.

Rosebud Ben-Oni

IN COLLEGE I remember a professor telling me that writers like Gloria Anzaldúa and Americo Paredes were "supplemental" and not necessary to understand the Western Canon, much less American Literature. That they were "regional" writers and wrote in specific dialects that did not accurately reflect the American experience at all. I also remember this same professor saying he had "read books about Mexico" and then citing D. H. Lawrence's *The Plumed Serpent* and Malcolm Lowry's *Under the Volcano*. He could not see the problem with that thinking . . .

*

Beware following a single north star that promises to carry you to poetry, entire. Now is rejecting a single, defining identity and single representation of "authoritative voice" in the now of US poetics. Single prevents the multi-singular unfolding of verse: I'm talking about stripping the canon of its role as the only starting point, as highest apex animal, for which to journey to Now. The now is the poet's encounter in all sorts of verisimilitudes, whether real time, physical encounters or virtual realities of FaceTime and *Poetry* podcasts, whether memory or dreams. The poet now is hungry and rarely satisfied with simple virtues and "poetry saves." The poet now is hungry for what realities picked apart, consumed and (re)created. The poet now is anthropophagist, the ever-adapter who absorbs and subverts the environments and its histories/physicalities/spirits around us. Now we aren't sure what's real, or who is the sum total of "we" and that kind of power, and all the ways poets are joined in those realities. Yet our poems, consumed together toward a bloodied whole, the feast of their contradictions, is how we find not one truth but the impact of our various encounters with the world and each other.

Phillip B. Williams

WE HAVE TO remember what has happened to all of our people. How do we create poems that allow us to be global citizens? I think it helps to use the facts as they appear without dressing them up or Americanizing them, meaning making subtext of all we write be about how it feels to be an American.

*

. . . which is why I have promised myself to read more translations. In thinking about Auden, I wonder if what he says is true if we consider the isolation encouraged by reading solely from one's national imagination. How could poetry make anything happen if it only feeds the status quo, if it's only written in order to push toward the known other than elucidating, as best as possible, the desire to express empathy, speak the unknown? To Adorno's point, I think I agree with him if I allow myself to manipulate what isn't said. I tend to think of his statement as "To write poetry, to write about beauty and the mundane daily activity that is observation, after Auschwitz is barbaric." Part of me feels as though, of course, this can be dissolved quite easily as illogical and pedantic, but there is something for me that is odd about reading a poem during a time when, worldwide, people are suffering, particularly when that poem seems to have no interest in the suffering of anyone at all. But we need all modes, forms, and interests and we need them simultaneously, much like we need the work of all nations.

Stephanie Burt

To SAY THAT there are things called lyric poems, and that they have common features from antiquity (even if they also diverge as history, and literary history, move on) is also to say that people and their inner lives have common features over time, and that poets describe them.

*

The word "poetry" (from poiesis, a word about making) means lots of things when you try to use it to cover verbal art forms, verbal makings, over a wide period of time (say, more than a generation). It used to mean "imaginative literature," including prose. It still means "a set of techniques, ways to use words in aid of imagination." Metaphor, for example. Impersonation. Line breaks. Enjambment. Rhyme. We use those techniques to all sorts of ends, these days, some of them mutually incompatible. Don't just ask "Is it a poem?" Ask what kind of poem it could be, and whether it's good, and for what, and how, and for whom. Then ask what all these techniques, what all these kinds of making, have in common. Maybe it's the presence of people who care for the sounds of words, and have something to say.

Birgit Mara Kaiser

THE PLANETARY SCOPE of literary production and reception, the weakening of the national as valid framework for the study of literature and a renewed awareness of poetics as transnational and intra-active urges us to recalibrate our practices of critical reading, comparison and translation. In view of the abundance of literary works beyond European languages and canonicity, the categories of national literatures and inter-national comparison are losing weight.

*

Poetics is infinitely small and infinitely large at the same time, and always in the plural.

It is infinitely large in that it makes happen—*poiesis* means making, as in: the unfolding of the world in its myriad ways, the production of world, intra-actively. It names the forces of becoming, planetarily entangled, challenging the order of narrative and discourse, the illusion of transcendental certainties. Faced with the facts of empire, Glissant's *Poetics of Relation* claims "poetic thought" : a thought that "beneath the fantasy of domination [. . .] sought the really livable world." The living and the livable.

And poetics is infinitely small, because it comes in syllables, sound-bites, turns of phrases, moves. It can take form as poetry, which also surfaces in prose. Defying generalization and abstraction, it is small as in: practiced and situated, stressing the singular material grounds of any utterance—this breath that speaks it, this sound that carries it, this phrase that turns musical. It demands attention for the opaque, the material, the singular.

And it is always plural. Poetics. Poetic thought, as Glissant writes, "safeguards the particular, since only the totality of truly secure particulars guarantees the energy of Diversity"—the fluctuating complexity of our planetary today.

Making

WE TAKE OUR measure of being from what surrounds us; and what surrounds us is always, to some extent, of our own making.

*

Making is not only material. Yes, we live in made houses and drive made cars, but we also think made thoughts and use words' made meanings and operate within made cultural understandings.

Poetry, too, is made, but it is also a making, and what it makes is what it is made of: all those thoughts and meanings and cultural understandings. And *that* doubleness (its making what it is made of) gives it another doubleness: it makes us, by whom it is made.

Rachel Blau DuPlessis

[I]T IS TIME for a totally different History of Poetry talking about "woman/women," "man/men," femininity, masculinity, sexuality, effeminacy, female masculinity, and queerness, torqueing and resisting binaries. Poetic traditions, genres of poems, poetic authority as textually manifested, representations of subjectivity and social location, discussions of relationships including romance, love, desire, inspiration, and repulsion—all elements deeply constitutive of poetic texts—can reveal gender assumptions that open the "field" of poetry to new ways of envisioning its purpose, problems of representation, and meanings.

*

The citation you've chosen from me and your general question are quite different. My cited words call for a critical act—analysis of gender in the field of poetry. Your general question asks what "must" (ick) or "might" poetry be "now," implicitly calling for summary statements in the manner of the considered *obiter dicta* from Auden and Adorno. Your question concerns *production*—even a program—modeling aphorisms of a skeptical poet and post-Holocaust cultural critic. My citation concerns *reception* and encourages literary critics to think about gender in poetry. I have (in fact) written "Draft 52: Midrash"—a twenty-seven-section, seventeen-page poem responding at length to what Adorno has said.

Because poetic work is hyper-saturated with its own

reverberating evocativeness, because poetry is saturated segmentivities in social-sensuous language, it will always manifest versions of the "now." The *now* occurs in vocabulary, jargons; the *now* emerges in tones and diction; the *now* occurs in topics that poets choose and allusions (formal, aesthetic, historical, traditional) that poems make.

Poetry is that form of writing that encourages the largest zones for excess of meanings and implications to infuse the text. In poetry, language does not simply produce a meaning—it prolongs multifarious meanings from its *now* into our *now*.

Robert Stewart

I AM SUGGESTING that there is a unity to all things. The kind of revelation I hoped to find in Paul had as much to do with connections as with ideas, with God as with thoughts about God. We have a choice. The appeal to a work of art—a book, a sculpture—rises from faith that the work represents more than information. Despite certain disappointments, each newly discovered book dangles before us a single possibility: that a human mind has found its expressive hanging garden, its Atlantis, its road to Damascus.

*

Auden's statement that "poetry makes nothing happen" happens to be of little help in life or art until one reads into the lines that follow, which hardly get any attention: "It [poetry] survives / in the valley of its making," Auden says; poetry is "A way of happening," which I take to mean that poetry is not to be left to winners or losers, as in war, 1939, executives or generals, or to madness—the holy squire of self-expression—but is [poetry] a made thing, given to literary precepts of unity, movement, honesty and completeness. The Zen masters say our objective is to look at, listen to, touch, and taste things. I am changed—as it happens—by reading Issa, "The man pulling radishes / pointed my way / with a radish." In its directness, the poem offers completeness, direction. It sets me off on the road. Robert Hass says, as well, that when a thing is seen clearly enough, there is a sense of absence about it. It [poetry] contains, in itself, everything. I would suggest, in these terms, that it occurs as a work of beauty.

Oren Izenberg

POETRY, PERHAPS NOT alone, but to a high degree among the arts, dwells in multiple temporalities. Poetic responses to contingency are influenced by non-contingent entailments of the medium; the fact that a poem is a made thing that is heard, read, or seen motivates its perennial interest in problems of voice and address, substance and its perception. Such concerns are not just critical fantasies about or impositions upon poems, but common objects of poets' own conscious deliberation—whatever forms those deliberations take.

*

Poetry, if it is anything, is a made thing and, being made, it is made out of something. So, whatever it can be may only be achieved in negotiation with whatever it must be. We can do with words (to pick one thing that poetry can be made from) only everything that *words* can do.

Likewise, persons (if they are anything) are made of something; what they can be is only achieved as a negotiation with what they must be. We can do with minds (to pick one thing that persons can be made from) only anything that *minds* can do.

This very basic likeness between poems and persons has been—and in my view can only continue to be—very productive for poetic thinking: Auden, provoked by Yeats's extreme wishes for a poetry that might remake the individual soul or restore the national one—is interested in thinking about what words can't do (make the mortal immortal, and the imperfect perfect) and about what they can (memorialize through praise of imperfection). Adorno, provoked by what he understands as the extreme consequence of human reason in Auschwitz, declares what persons can't do (absolve reason of its guilt by making beautiful words) as a way of expanding our thinking about what persons must be (thus his notion of a "nonidentical" consciousness which might negate the dominating force of human rationality).

What might be said about poetry? What can be said: "Poetry" is what we tend to call our ongoing negotiations with whatever we perceive to be ("now") the non-negotiable conditions of being anything at all. This is why it will never end (negotiation with the world never ends)—or, properly speaking, begin (the world does not negotiate).

Stuart Cooke

[T]HERE IS AN enormous lacuna in Australian literary studies about the relationship of contemporary Aboriginal poetry to traditional forms of songpoetry. This relates to a larger, more willful ignorance of the relationship between the *voice* of the poet and the *text* that is printed on the page . . . [T]o separate these two modalities is to deny the importance of much of the Aboriginal poetic tradition . . . Once we discard the European notion of a "poem" as a purely text-based object that one studies in literature departments at universities, we can begin to appreciate the truly multimedia complex of the songpoem.

*

What I want to say is to do with gesture. What I want to do is build a frame, establish a territory of some kind, inscribe a surface. But who knows where or how this might take place? As I write a poem I also write over vestiges of song (the lyre), of design (orthography), of an ecological ontology (I am; it is; these things; etc.). But this has little to do with the marks themselves, or with the pen or keyboard or voice recorder that distributes them. Without hands, the poem rushes into song and the ephemeral inscriptions of dance: the Albert's Lyrebird, for example, who taps sticks in time with his song, for whom cycles, rather than lines, constitute size, object, territory; he manipulates vines so that the foliage shimmers, ripples of light lining the dark (a forest text). Now I return to the composition of a poem in accordance with its place in Country, to its recital amongst dance and music and painting, or to the way a Nyigina man from the West Kimberley might draw symbols in the dirt to accompany the language from his mouth (poetry splitting into two channels: the finger; the tongue). I am interested more in the modulations of textures, and in a need to conjugate those around with those within, than I am in this crystalline word or that concrete phrase.

Ailish Hopper

[R]ACE IN AMERICA is just like bad fiction, with one-dimensional characters, predictable plotlines, passive verbs, subjectless sentences. Even our remedy-stories constrain, or can, if they too become more narratives to be race-patrolled; stories of heroism or helplessness, identities that become narrow containers. Yet it is possible to rewrite, meaning not merely to "revise," but write poems that neither ignore racial codes nor give over their power to them. Poems that . . . expand our vision of ourselves—all that we are, all that we are not—to introduce the "another world," as Paul Éluard supposedly put it, that's "in this one."

*

Poetry is a force. I don't think we, especially in the US, have the slightest idea of what it's capable of. Certainly we haven't seen the fullness, yet, of the kind and types of forms it can give rise to.

I don't defer to Auden and Adorno. But I offer my respect, and use what's inside their words—what is art, but working with constraints?—for worlds they might never have imagined.

James D. Sullivan

[I]N ORDER TO encounter a poem, we must read it or hear it in a richly coded material setting. Somebody is reciting it, or it appears as a published artifact . . . By reading poetry as a cultural practice, as something people do—rather than as a series of abstractable texts, linguistic constructs removable from any material contest—we can see that, as poetry gets passed around, it is necessarily a heteroglot practice.

*

Poetry is something people do. They write it, think it, recite it, hear it, share it, send it off to little magazines while crossing their fingers, judge it, edit it, design graphic or audio context for it, post it on Facebook or Tumblr, condemn it, critique it, get jobs or tenure on account of it, toss away other parts of their lives to devote themselves to it, read it alone because they love it or in classroom groups because teachers make them read it, print it, publish it, advertise it, ignore it, use an excerpt to support or make vivid some argument, buy it, forget it, or let it color all the rest of their lives. The same text means a different thing to each of these people and in each of these transactions. Except in one of those physical interactions, it's inert. It lives only as people do things with it. So when you do something with a poem, make it something cool.

Ed Bok Lee

AT THE DEEPEST substratum of all poetry, it seems to me, aches the interconnectedness of everything.

*

The poem will remember you.

But it's easy to forget this. People do it all the time, and get brutalized by the emptiness of their lives.

Fortunately, the poem is always, eternally here—to access, to fill you with the living stream.

I think it has to do with why Aristotle noted that, in the final analysis, Poetry is more important than History. Everything else is something still not yet accrued to even the semblance of a poem—some authentic remaking—and so lags in a far away land of arbitrary and extensive decorations of and for the dead.

Reimagine

THE MODERN ARTIST is less a creator than a discoverer of the as yet unseen, the inventor of the previously unimagined that only emerges into reality through him.

*

No one takes the reason as objectless, operating in a vacuum, arriving at conclusions ex nihilo. Why the imagination? We would come closer to describing the actual capacity if we thought of it as re-imagination, a remaking of something given, not the production of something out of a hat or "out of thin air." Doing so would make it easier to see the existential significance of imagination, as what enables me to recalibrate and reorient and refresh and reconstruct myself, make of my given self a new self.

Lesley Wheeler

MANY WRITERS . . . RENDER the lyric poem as a house, a kind of enclosure. However . . . , this conception of the lyric has been particularly evocative for women writers, because of the profound and often-remarked association between women and the domestic sphere . . . The genre of the lyric obliges [the] "need for secrecy" as do Gaston Bachelard's enclosing drawers, chests, and wardrobes; paradoxically, it also can offer immense interiors, more free than exterior prisons.

*

I wrote the lines above at a different moment in history and in my own life, but I still understand a powerful poem as an alternate possible spacetime: I read myself over the threshold and may be transformed by what I experience there. That isn't to define the lyric as an escape from suffering or politics. After all, even the most transported reader or listener has to return to the pain in her body, rising sea levels, pervasive violence. Poetry can, however, cast an estranging light over a traveler, redefining what matters. It might even help some of us imagine a kinder, saner way of inhabiting the world.

Diane Glancy

POETRY EXAMINES AN emotional truth. It's an experience filtered through the personality of the poet. We look to poetry for visions, not scientific truths. The poet's job is to combine new elements. Explore their melting, seeping into one another. The metaphor is the building block of the poem. It & sound. Narrative doesn't always do it anymore.

Poetry saves what is human in this world going gaudy & insane.

*

Subversion of the Apparent

To say that poetry is poetry is to unfence the field—and that what is said straightforwardly can be obliterated. Poetry is the act of itself in abstraction and sometimes annihilation of the evident. Poetry is a narrative of inversion. Subtext as text. A reticence of meaning. Poetry bypasses the areas around the statements of explanation, and presents its attributes. Its annals in the dark. The qualities of the intangible. That is poetry. The non-saying of the saying. I watched a program on Medieval Gothic cathedrals. When early architects learned how to hold up massive ceilings with arches instead of walls, light became a building material. The great stained windows did not have to bear utilitarian weight, but could be glass that transcended into the field.

Unfenced. Poetry is called forthwith to say around the edges. To balance with attributes. The building material of light.

Alicia Suskin Ostriker

WHAT THEN IS important in contemporary women's poetry? What follows from women's cultural marginality and their equivocal relation to a canon that they appropriate, resist, and transform? First of all, there is the discovery that marginality, however painful, may be artistically useful. Some linked motifs announce themselves: the quest for self-definition, the body, the eruption of anger, the equal and opposite eruption of eros, the need for revisionist mythmaking.

*

I have to say these words of mine feel very old-fashioned. *Stealing the Language* was published in 1986, and this little passage summarizes its argument. It's nice to think that we have really moved on. Women are mainstream now. So what's new? I think Cave Canem has changed the course of the river, and that the best, liveliest, strongest, most confident, most varied and most moving poetry in America today is being written by Afro-American poets. What's next?

Anis Shivani

NOTHING'S WRONG WITH poetry. Everything's wrong with the "poets" who come at it like a career, with a sense of instrumentality and pragmatism. Poetry comes from inspiration, experience, mysticism, vision, ecstasy, transcendence, clairvoyance, prophecy, apocalypticism, decadence, misery, eroticism, not from sitting in a classroom with your bourgeois concerns about sex and relationships, and giving it a semblance of art with the acquisition of "craft" taught by masters of the profession . . . No one in the real world gives a damn about poetry, and that's as it should be, because of the abysmal narcissistic product coming out of the system.

*

Auden and Adorno's statements are probably the twentieth century's two most quoted—and most misunderstood—propositions about poetry, along with William Carlos Williams's "no ideas but in things," all of which parallel Philip Roth's lifelong denial of the possibility of fiction. Ironic that Auden, identified with the left-wing activist generation of the 1930s, should say what he did, and ironic that Adorno, who wanted to take aesthetic theory to a new level, should say what he did. Both are true at the level of utter banality, in the sense that truisms are, but not true when we start thinking about them. Poetry makes nothing happen was meant to suggest not to expect the material reality of the world to change because of poetry, but even at that level it's not true because those who open themselves to humanist ideas do often change for the better and the world changes for the better in turn. Poetry changes everyone, to the extent that they're capable of improvement, and this becomes more true as we expand the definition of poetry beyond formal verse of the academic kind: so much more is poetry than we give it credit for. The idea that those who committed barbarities were exposed to poetry and music and went ahead with their monstrosities anyway seems to me one of the more fatuous arguments of our times. Mussolini had pretensions of being a violinist and wrote fiction but the degree of his barbarity had nothing to do with the sincerity of his appreciation for the arts. Consider too that he was relatively lax toward censorship of the arts compared to the Nazi regime. Also that he saw his country as a blank canvas upon which to reimagine the Italian people in poetic terms. Adorno is making the close connection between technicized barbarity and modernist high art, but it is a connection whose pursuit leads to dead-ends of thought. "No poetry after Auschwitz" (this is how Adorno's actual statement has become reframed in my imagination and of others) is meant to suggest that human barbarity has reached such levels that art is inadequate to capturing it. This is a ridiculous proposition; if anything can—and must—try to capture the dark side of humanity, it is poetry and fiction. Consider Charles Johnson's *Middle Passage* or Cormac McCarthy's *The Road*, or John Berryman's *Dream Songs* or Amiri Baraka's *Preface to a Twenty Volume Suicide Note*, and tell me that there is no poetry after Auschwitz (or any real or imagined apocalypse). These propositions have become a cudgel for those in arts bureaucracies (among whom I would include most reviewers and critics) who wish to see an end to poetry that does make things happen, i.e., not in the immediate policy sense but in raising human consciousness. It has been true of the American imperial project since at least the intervention in World War II to see an end to threatening art, as part of the pacification of minds that is supposed to make the world safe for American-style capitalism. Thus the duplicity that "to write poetry after Auschwitz is barbaric" assumes a more sinister dimension, even if it was Adorno who said it. Roth, who wrote fiction for sixty years and yet kept saying that no one reads it, represents those whose interest it is to see art that makes things happen is extinguished. It's as if Don Draper of *Mad Men*, the most suave of ad men, were to say, "Advertising doesn't make people buy anything." True, but fundamentally untrue, and obscurantist. My earlier statement about time-servers in the academic poetry world, who write poetry according to the presupposition that "poetry makes nothing happen" or "no poetry after Auschwitz," hints at the larger problem with human consciousness: the self-imposed limits to imagination, which are very much part of how people are governed today. Foucault is more on point for having perceived the degree to which people commit themselves to self-limiting discourse—such as discourse about the function of art—in a way that makes it difficult or impossible to alter the terms of the discourse. But true poets always redefine the aesthetic preconditions, and conditions of reception, upon which their discipline is supposed to rest. So Foucault, too, is wrong at the fundamental level. Discourse is pliable, malleable, individualized to the atomic level, at least potentially so, therefore shaping and reshaping it is the most noteworthy thing that happens, and keeps happening with each original utterance. Poetry can't help but make things happen. And no poetry *before* Auschwitz. Those would be my counter-assertions.

Melissa Girard

WHEN THE NEW Critics professionalized literary criticism, they simultaneously deprofessionalized a rich critical and aesthetic discourse produced by women poets in the modern era. When we followed the New Critics and left Bogan, Millay, Taggard, and Wylie behind, we lost a canon of once prominent modernist poets. But this canonical thinning, however significant, is only one aspect of our impoverishment. More fundamentally . . . , we lost an aesthetic method—a set of theories, values, and strategies for reading that arose from within that poetry, that made sense and meaning out of it. We lost, in other words, its poetics.

*

In looking back on the poetry of the past, we are often seeking affirmation. We want to see ourselves reflected back across a great expanse of time. This desire is human, but it limits our historical encounters. It makes much of the poetry of the past appear dull, because it doesn't shine with our own tastes, values, and beliefs. I am drawn to poetics that we have forgotten how to read or value: poems that seem too complicated or too simple, abstruse or prosaic, sterile or sentimental. In these poems that no longer quite reach us, there are traces of other ways of being, other reasons for valuing the poetic, which might be used to reform our present. These historical poetics are luminous.

Sandra María Esteves

THE POET IS a truth bearer of reality and image. We live in a society of denial that doesn't want to see or hear these truth tales, so consequently poets are shunned to a great degree because people don't always want to hear the truth . . . Sometimes being a poet can be dangerous and unwelcome territory.

*

Electric Poets
for Patricia Spears Jones

Old school with Aquarian tools,
some traditions in revision
in tune with time
to see in the dark
where we spark chronic electronics:
cell phones and lap tops—
digital toys are not all we've got.
We ride the cyber river
to find some place in space
between micro and macro,
alone, but still in need of touch.

Alone in the electronic rush,
another quasar fizzles into cosmic dust.
Our web presence will become

epithets on ethereal tombstones,
virtual monuments
to bear witness to our existence
that in this moment we choose
a path through our dreams
where ideas take form
and begin to breathe
with poems giving birth
repeatedly reaching
into alternate ways of seeing
like breaking bread
and clear water for drinking.

Gary Lenhart

To SPEAK ABOUT class in the United States, we must invent a way to do it that distinguishes our fluid situation from rigid European structures, but does not ignore that the most successful democratic movements in this country in the last fifty years (civil rights, feminism, gay and lesbian liberation) opened the managerial class and helped reduce discrimination within it, but failed to minimize the expanding gap between classes that has produced the most alarming, and burgeoning, symbol of class strife in America—the gated community . . . The major obstacle to discussing class and poetry is the lack of vocabulary.

*

Despite increased attention in our society to income inequality, what I wrote ten years ago about poetry and social class remains the case. We must find a way to say what we want. If the poem rings true, maybe someone will hear and respond. Or maybe they will find some other pleasure there that makes life more attractive. I remember looking at a painting of cars on West End Avenue and trying to understand what was wrong with the tires. Then one day as I was crossing the street I glanced down West End and saw that the tires were as in the painting. The feeling that my eyes were cleaned of dross remained for hours. At other times, instead of being stone cold sober, I enjoy a dreamy buzz.

I also recall a young woman getting very angry when I mentioned the historical context of a poem. She preferred to believe that all things were eternal and apparent. Her attitude was democratic, in that she thought everyone had the same feelings, but oppressively indifferent to individual experience and temperament. Our responses to poetry coincided occasionally, when qualities of sound, image, or thought struck our distinct fancies.

Kim Addonizio

HERE IS WHAT I believe, if this constitutes a poetics: I believe language was developed over millions of years as a way to communicate. Personally, I'm not interested in destroying meaning or multiplying it *ad infinitum*. I believe in narrative, in story. I believe in the lyric, that it is possible to sing. I believe that poetry is an act of consciousness and that most critics miss the point completely . . . Artists create out of their ideas, their obsessions, their interests, their passions, their lived and imaginative experience . . . Art is a function of the human spirit.

*

"If you want a picture of the future, imagine a boot stamping on a human face—forever." —George Orwell, *1984*. We are rapidly losing our freedoms and our privacies. Orwell understood that the most important colonization is mental. How to keep Big Brother out of our heads? That's the question for poets, for language and culture, for all of us. When our imaginative capacities are destroyed, the battle is lost.

Left

THE INFINITE THEN cannot be tracked down like game by a hunter. The trace left by the infinite is not the residue of a presence; its very glow is ambiguous.

*

In grief, we attach great importance to remnants. This was my father's pocket knife. This photo was taken three days before my beloved's death.

Insofar as (in Wallace Stevens's words) "The world is ugly, / And the people are sad," poetry can offer consolation, remain present even though I have lost what I have lost, and must lose soon what I have not lost yet.

Margaret Randall

FEAR AND MISTRUST make the strongest walls of all. Walls that keep out and walls that contain, spawning a hatred that diminishes those on both sides. Silence, cowardice, and conformity keep the walls standing. Our challenge is to pierce these structures, give voice to memory, revive and reignite history. A single voice may inspire a chorus.

*

I say today that I take exception to Auden's assertion that "poetry makes nothing happen." When it works, poetry can make everything happen. Adorno's affirmation, ten years later, that "to write poetry after Auschwitz is barbaric" was not, I don't believe, an absolute. Rather, it was a way of saying that what was perpetrated at Auschwitz was so horrendous it made evocation or any attempt at description fall short. Today, more than six decades after Auschwitz, we have so many other atrocities we cannot begin to enumerate them: the Killing Fields of Cambodia, the hundreds of thousands of Disappeared during the Dirty Wars of Latin America, Bosnia, Israel's unending war against the Palestinians, Rwanda, Sudan, the ravages of Mexico's drug cartels, fanatical Islam, the terrorized lives of Black youth and men across these United States. Poetry is our voice. It is what we have left. If it cannot give us wings to fly, we are doomed. Both horror and kindness render linear time and space meaningless. Poetry, when it works, creates a new timeline, a multiplicity of relevant spaces.

Rupert Loydell

IT IS THIS personalized moment, this perhaps selfish kind of evo-
cation, I am drawn to; it is only the author's clear sense of involve-
ment and location within the poem that in the end draws me to
poems. I believe that the most personal and intimate poetry is the
poetry that can say the most: by focusing we actually allow the
small-scale, the precious, to expand out into a shared readership.

*

I see the quote you have chosen is perhaps another "me", from
an old interview, one I do not totally recognize. These days I
would turn it round and say that a poet is in her work however
it is composed or constructed, but I do not want ego, experience
and epiphany as the focus of any text. Nothing must or has to be
said about poetry, it is its elusive and often obscure nature that
allows poetry to say almost anything in (m)any different ways.
The fact that it often makes nothing happen is poetry's strength,
as is the possibility that it might or sometimes does make some-
thing happen. Maybe this is what I meant by small-scale and a
poem's relationship with readers? I am interested in the struggle
I have to compose and locate myself in my own poems, because
they are assembled from the world around me: conversations,
quotations, discarded and ephemeral language. I am a kind of
sieve, and my poems are part of the filtration process I use to
survive. This sounds far grander than my writing process and
experience of poetry. Writing is not barbaric, it is all we have.

Jee Leong Koh

I'M FLYING TONIGHT to the country to which I could have migrated but did not. For personal and historical reasons, the UK is the natural home for my work. The British understand where I come from, without too much explanation; they understand too my resistances and ambivalences as a postcolonial subject. In contrast, the Americans, by and large, don't even understand that they are an empire.

*

When I moved into my Upper West Side apartment in February 2011, I found a sheaf of haiku in the bedroom closet. To my surprise, the poet made numerous references to people and places that I knew from living in New York City. I was thus compelled to translate the poems from the Japanese. As I worked on these exhilarating, enigmatic pieces, I found myself searching out the street corner, the tree, and even the bird that had so enraptured our poet. In this manner I traced the route that he or she must have often taken through Central Park—entering at 86th Street on the west side, then running south of the reservoir, or else strolling north of the Great Lawn by the Arthur Ross pinetum, finally exiting on the east side at either 84th or 85th Street. Slowly but surely I was beginning to live the life glimpsed through these haiku. I now walk in the poet's footsteps every day to where I teach school. Here's an American haiku by one who signed off as "an insignificant Japanese poet."

You can say
anything in a haiku
except fuck you

Mary Ruefle

METAPHOR IS NOT, and never has been, a mere literary term. It is an event. *A poem must rival a physical experience* and metaphor is, simply, an exchange of energy between two things. If you believe that metaphor is an event, and not just a literary term denoting comparison, then you must conclude that a certain philosophy arises: the philosophy that everything in the world is connected. I'll go slowly here: if metaphor is not an idle comparison, but an exchange of energy, an event, then it unites the world by its very premise—that things connect and exchange energy.

*

I have no new words to add to this statement because I still believe it. That said, I would make it clearer that metaphor does not exist in the world at large (outside of ourselves) but exists as a perception—an event—that arises spontaneously in our minds, which are hardwired to think figuratively. We ourselves cause the "event" of metaphor. What a powerful capacity we have, to be able to connect and unite things using only our minds. Still, the world's a mess. That's because the mind is capable of other things, too, terrible things counter to a positive exchange of energy.

And if a poem didn't rival a physical experience, who on earth would bother reading them? I would have stopped long ago.

I do not think that anything must or might be said about poetry *now* that could not have been said on the afternoon of its birth. The vernacular changes, and with it the style, but that's about it, and none of it essential—it would be like saying teeth weren't teeth before the advent of dentistry. I agree with Auden. But surely readers know he had in mind the Big Picture, the complex and fraught social world; poetry can indeed impact the life of an individual—I know it impacted mine and changed it forever—but it can make nothing happen on the scale Auden had in mind. If it could, after Hopkins wrote "Binsley Poplars" we would have stopped chopping down trees! No, poetry makes nothing happen, but as it continues to have a wondrously delirious impact on individual psyches, I'm all for it. The Adorno statement is slippery; it depends on whether you interpret it to mean that poetry can't be written, or that it's simply barbaric if it is. Plenty of poems have been written since Auschwitz, just as they continued to be written after the countless holocausts prior to the Second World War. So on that hand he's disproven, but then we are left with the question Is all this poetry barbaric? Maybe it is, maybe Whitman's "barbaric yawp" (is that it?) is all any of us have. So what? Long live the futility of the artist. Fail better, as has been said. And lastly, if I were in a concentration camp and were to be executed, the last thing I would want to hear is that all art would perish from the earth because of my death, because of man's inhumanity to man. What kind of memorial is that? I would want to hear that afar off someone was safe from what was happening to me, and that someone was having a good day, and making art.

Anne Simpson

[W]E HAVE TO be alert to the dangers of a world split apart. A vision of all-encompassing unity allows us to see the world as an ecological web in which we are participants. Metaphor, like geometry, shows us how to be open to such unity . . . Whether we are poets or mathematicians, artists or philosophers, our work is to be alive to, and reveal correspondences within, this elegantly complex, richly varied, and resonant structure.

*

When the poet Paul Celan—a Romanian Jew who lost his parents in the Holocaust—won the Bremen Prize for German Literature in 1958, he said that only language had remained through searing losses: "But it had to go through its own lack of answers, through the terrifying silence, through the thousand darknesses of murderous speech. It went through . . . and could resurface, 'enriched' by it all." That it resurfaced at all is miraculous, but that it resurfaced enriched is testament to its power.

Yet poetry holds no power in the usual sense: it doesn't make things happen, nor does it make sense of the world. Its work is to witness for that which has no voice, to speak the unspeakable, and to show us what we have not yet imagined. This *could* be that, it says. Your experience *could* be my experience, it says. It refuses to be diminished or destroyed. In this sense, the present time (whether now or in the future) is always the most important time for poetry to do what it does best—to enlarge us by opening us up to what is possible.

Farid Matuk

KAIROS IS A visionary [rhetorical] strategy in that it requires one to step, if only slightly, outside of ideology or of dominant modes of perception in order to make these into tools. If archive fever always excludes as it includes, then artists and poets using *kairos* can not only choose the optimal time to deploy an argument, they can also spur audiences into making the excluded "documents" legible.

*

Cathy Park Hong said something about comedy being the art of making vomit come out as laughter. Maybe lyric poetry is the art of making vomit come out as wonder? What representations, tactical satires, or conceptual gestures need to pile up around us to destroy whiteness, and if whiteness is destroyed, to what will I react? Do you remember what Henry Watson's body looked like when it lifted above the intersection of Florence and Normandy to kick Reginald Denny's white head and beautiful hair? It was flying.

It is 2015, the sun is shining and the sky is behaving itself. I live near an Air Force base. Young pilots practice takeoffs and landings in A-10 attack planes, in massive carriers and fighter jets too. Of course I'm sympathetic with Palestinians and any contained and policed people in a casual way. But when I think of committing my body for the sake of anybody, I taste vomit. I guess flying feels good. I just know I don't have to do it myself. That's how my poem ends. But I'm trying to let the vomit go and follow that arc.

Form

IF YOU HAVE a clear idea of a soul, you will also have a clear idea of a form; for it is of the same genus, though a different species.

*

Poetry cannot replicate the forms in nature, including the human (physical or spiritual) form. It can, though, and does and *must*, replicate their formedness.

Robert Sheppard

I WANT TO define poetics quite precisely as a speculative writerly discourse, developed by writers themselves. Poetics is the product of the process of writers' reflections upon writing, and upon their acts of writing, gathering from the past and from others, and casting into the future, speculatively and conjecturally, even provocatively on occasions. Poetics exists for the writer and for others in a hoped for writerly community, to produce, to quote Rachel Blau DuPlessis, a "permission to continue". It involves a theory of practice, a practice of theory—its conjectures are often provisional, its trajectory nomadic, its positions temporary.

*

The Formal Splinter

Poems both say and do not say, modified by formal resistance and interruption. The critical function of the work of art is asserted by it being art, by it having form at all. By being form. A poem doesn't (just) say, it can't be paraphrased; it participates, criticizes by operating a critique of itself in self-reflection. Poems—critical in their forms and forming—act. Form may be *sedimented* content, yet is cognitive, since form is material engagement, cognition embedded in sedimentation and in the critical function that is itself called into being by form (and its autonomy). Dissensus (rather than consensus, both socially and artistically) produces the manifold devices of formally investigative poetry (including that poetry now rather widely called linguistically innovative): varieties of montage and de-montage emphasizing disruption, interruption, imperfect fit and unfinish, as well as transformation and transposition, creative linkage. They put disorder at the heart of art's order, while simultaneously putting order at the heart of its disruption. Resisting signification within signification is the formal splinter at, and in, the heart of the poem. Its critical function is born in the instant art's form de-forms and re-forms in front of us as precisely a representation of freedom.

—2015

Timothy Steele

WHAT IS MOST essential to human life and to its continuance remains a love of nature, an enthusiasm for justice, a readiness of good humor, a spontaneous susceptibility to beauty and joy, an interest in our past, a hope for our future, and, above all, a desire that others should have the opportunity and encouragement to share these qualities. An art of measured speech nourishes these qualities in a way no other pursuit can.

*

Given the prestige of the modern sciences, it was perhaps inevitable that modern poetry would look to them for a model of cumulative progress based on experiment and technical innovation. But that model has not always served poetry well because its function differs from science's. While both science and poetry benefit from intellectual rigor and honesty, science illuminates principles of the physical universe, whereas poetry addresses human experience. Where science involves quantitative matters, poetry attends to qualitative issues involving the social, ethical, political, and psychological conditions under which we live. While scientists can win assent by demonstrable truths, poets offer more provisional judgments about our lives and conduct. Poets must consider style as much as substance. They must speak compellingly to move an audience. Hence the perennial value of rhetoric and metrics: they help make language memorable and exciting.

All poets should write as they wish, and we should respect all forms of poetry. But maybe we should avoid getting caught up in the rush of self-superseding technologies and fashions that occupied so many poets in the twentieth century. Maybe it's time to think a little less about making it new and a little more about making it good.

Sean Hill

Because I tend to spend most of my time above water, literally at least, I see more birds than fish . . . Like poems, they move through space, turning and plunging, and live in the air—but poems are articulated by teeth, tongue, lips, and breath. Joints are articulations, and poems have those in a manner of speaking.

*

Patterning

Poems are explorations and articulations of the worlds we live in; they are made things—artifacts. Poems are systems of patterns like the seasons or sweeping shoals of fish; we fashion them from life using language—that patterning technology that allows us to communicate, think abstractly, relate concrete details, and shape our realities. A poem has form, a shape like a tree or a gun, and that's what engages us—the patterns of sounds and rhythms in the air and images in our minds and lines on the page. Poems are connections and resolutions and complications. A poem is and has articulation—putting into words ideas or feelings and the state of being jointed. Poems are necessary—I need to write at least one poem in which I consider what if anything joins Plessy v. Ferguson to Michael Brown and Ferguson, MO. That is and has been part of the now I'm joined to and must deal with as much as trees, the seasons, guns, and fish. Perhaps in that poem

I will need to explore and articulate the connections there and with any number of things.

Roo Borson

POETRY IS MADE of words, yet it is exactly as articulate as music, and as distinct from ordinary speech. (Remember High School's floundering attempts to paraphrase good literature? In the end, the honest will resort to a sputtering, insistent recitation of the original.) The motion of thought is its real melody, spoken in a near monotone. Poor poetry, I want to say—fluteless, impoverished. But it is still beautifully cantabile.

*

Poetry, for me, has been a slow education. In the seductiveness of patterned sound. In sensory imagery as a relatively direct mode of thought. In the cryptic encoding and decoding of experience. Ultimately in the exhilarating and unexpected transmissions of thought, fact, and feeling that are not only made possible through poetry, but are irrepressible in it.

Sandra Lim

[T]HERE IS NOT much poetry from which I feel excluded. I don't imagine myself above personal identifications (I'm hardly color-blind), but I might have to insist upon a lack of allegiance, upon my prerogative to have a multiple sensibility. My ideal is for the poetic imagination as violent and marvelous free space, a space to think and feel without stinting, to court ideological inconsistency, to express feelings of (at times dire) cultural contingency.

*

There is a consistent through-line here: a marveling at poetry's inherent capacity to change and change again, or rather, to dynamically counter its own self-possession at every turn. It appears to be one of the most powerful and paradoxical things about the art form. And the uses of form, whether they are political, aesthetic, evidentiary, seem rooted in the fact that form is so obviously a linguistic, and not a psychological, question. And so, poetic form makes potentiality come associatively, erotically, restlessly alive. Giorgio Agamben clarifies this sense of becoming in language: "A subjectivity is produced where the living being, encountering language and putting itself into play in language without reserve, exhibits in a gesture the impossibility of its being reduced to this gesture."

Particularity

THE WORLD ENTERS the work as it enters our ordinary lives, not as worldview or system, but in sharp particularity.

*

We keep trying to say something general about poetry, *I* keep trying to. But maybe there is nothing of the sort to be said. Maybe poetry hosts only particularity, is itself only in particular. Always ready to be spoken, never available to be spoken of.

Christian Wiman

ART IS NOT life, and life is not art, but they face each other like two jagged matching cliffs that look as if they were once together, but with a long, long fall between them now.

*

I don't believe in poetry. Both Auden's and Adorno's statements are nonsensical to me. That abstraction—poetry—is always a lie, especially when it is press-ganged into service for useless truths like these.

However. I do believe in poems. And their existential efficacy, even in the face of absolute desolation. I'm thinking of Miguel Hernandez's "Lullaby of the Onion," Chidiock Tichborne's "Elegy," Paul Celan's "Deathfugue," Miklós Radnóti's "Postcards." I choose these extreme examples to match up with Auden's and Adorno's apparently extreme statements, which the poems neither ratify nor refute. They just expose such portentousness for what it is.

And those cliffs? (Speaking of portentousness . . .) I don't remember writing that sentence and think I'll skip looking it up. Abstractions, abstractions, abstractions—nothing to build on there.

Darren Bifford

[T]HERE IS A particular resonance of metaphorical thinking (call it: poetic practice) with the development of a cogent ecological sensibility: by asserting the existence of relationships between things that, spoken non-metaphorically, are unrelated, metaphor facilitates the deep acknowledgement of a diversity of forms of life. Because that acknowledgement is predicated on an open form of attention—"a kind of love"—we are enabled to order our own commitments in a way appropriate to the variety of insight various metaphors engender.

*

I'm reticent to offer any general statement about what poetry is or does or might be. This is because poems, in their procedures and effects, are always particular. So what we might say now about poetry that we haven't in the past, either in defense of its quixotic lyrical traditions, or to articulate some other poetic form, seems to me little beyond the act of writing the poems we wish to write and offering them up to whoever might be listening. Which reminds me of that famous line in Auden's elegy to Yeats, that poetry makes nothing happen. It's too often read in the universal key, cast adrift as if it were an aphorism. Omitted is the fact that Auden offers the line as a premise in a specific context: the country whose troubles hurt Yeats into the composition of *Easter, 1916* has, sadly, its madness still, and Yeats's poetry did not make that madness sane—but it nonetheless survives "In

the valley of its making [as . . .] A way of happening, a mouth".
That distinction—between poetry as a making and poetry as a
way—is crucial. Of course I puzzle over Auden's meaning but I
suspect it is resonant with the claim that poems speak for them-
selves; that is enough.

Andrea Brady

[A]LTHOUGH PLEASURE IS a vital part of our aesthetic experience, its elaboration by theory has never seemed really adequate. In comparison, the attribution of meanings to difficult poetry seems easy enough . . .

*

My poems engage in the prosodic regulation of freedom and plenitude. Both sides of the equation are fantastic. Poets often tell us that formal bondage is an impediment to the creative indulgence of their will, and critics say the opposite: that the rule, emerging progressively like democracy, guarantees the mind's pleasant indiscipline. My current work supposes that neither of these things are true, that confinement is not a general metaphysical condition of which actual incarceration is a special case, for alongside the poet's masque of constraint there are other poets in actual fetters. What poetry makes happen depends on who it's happening to, and in what rooms. Solitude is both a privileged space where sentimental citizenship can reflect upon itself, and a punitive technology.

I experience other people's poems as miraculous determinations of the unsaid, the unrealized thing tricked out of history. That's pleasure. I experience my own poems as frustrating simulacra of their own impulses; sometimes as kind or dangerous or exquisite memories anchored in details that weren't actually there; always as failures. That's dissatisfaction. Both chemicals are required for the catalyzing of more poems. I am trying to dredge up this peculiar pleasure, maybe I had it on the cement steps out front, and the arc the plane took between the uprights that gripped the power cables for the R7 local. But can it be cold-pressed into service? I am trying to be granular. I am trying to be the grains that are the particularities of these instances, the people and their heels, the pixilated weather, so I can be held by them as the poems are. Abel says, we are up in space, because the ball we're on is in space. I am trying to get his space into poems, to hold the grains and the cables. This is a difficult compression, the earth merely a component.

Sophie Mayer

[IN WORKS BY Indigenous writers in the genre Dean Rader has named the "epic lyric,"] [h]istory, memory, and genealogy—the material of epic—are interlinked with precise, localized observations of the living world as it interpenetrates the poet's embodiment, senses, emotions, and memories. The phrasing is inadequate: English, with its strict distinction of subject and object by sentence order, lacks either verbs or pronouns to indicate the mutual constitution of observer, observing, and observed in an Indigenous poem.

These poets, however, bend English, insistent that—as a language born of the body and the world—it must be able to speak of this mutuality and interdependence; English's authority is thus destabilized.

*

Why is it only the Sho'ah that creates a condition of unspeakability for Adorno? Why not colonialism and its attempted (and continuing) genocides? That's my first thought about the juxtaposition of this quotation with the "key texts" from Adorno and Auden. The second, relatedly, is how Eurocentric these authors are in their apprehension of "poetry." If anything can be said about poetry now, it's that such a universalizing worldview—and such a poetry—is redundant. Poetry now (insofar as poetry is an open entity rather than a closed canon) is a poetry of specificities in which a new aesthetics of mutuality could be founded, what

Joan Retallack calls a "poethics." Its bend and stretch is found in the voices that have been most silenced and had to be most innovative and thoughtful in forging a poetics, and have kept a faith that poetry makes something happen, if only (what an only) itself.

Frank Bidart

THE UNREALIZABLE IDEAL is to write as if the earth opened and spoke. I think that if the earth *did* speak, she would espouse no one set of values, affections, meanings, that everything embraced would also somehow be annihilated and denied.

*

This morning, after tinkering with it for days, I wrote this:

You, Early, Knew You

were gay—asked if giving or getting a blowjob
felt better, you (who had known neither) knew.

Whether this is good or bad or stupid or simply opaque and willed, I don't know. Maybe after living with it for a few days, I'll decide I can keep it or must bury it. The process of writing a poem, inextricably mixed up with judging it even as I first write a line, reflects every battered thing I have thought a poem now must or can be. Or a tiny bit, a shard of that thing. Reading Catullus I sense no difference between what poetry was for Catullus and what poetry can and must be for us. The prose we write about poems must try not to shrivel before the poems we write. Maybe in a few hours or days I'll regret I let anyone see this "poem."

Edward M. Pavlić

THE FUNDAMENTAL CONTRADICTION in modernist creative tech-
nique emerges when artists embrace a sort of "objective" dis-
tance to achieve a more immediate experience of the crossroads
where the world and the self meet . . . Several strains in African
American literature and culture adopt or adapt modernist tech-
niques to explore these fluid and tumultuous realities.

*

What poem? I'm eight. Listening to the radio, Michael, Marvin
or Chaka Khan, my body spilled into a voice, no matter the
mop, seeped through the cracks in historical planks. I'm getting
off a dhow at the lip of a sandy, deserted island off the coast near
the Somali border. Behind a woman with golden slippers and a
skintight dress with bite me printed all over it, I step onto the 5
train at E 180th Street in the Bronx. Holding Baldwin's *No Name
in the Street*, I walk into a classroom at the University of Georgia.
I'm on a bus in no-man's-land, crossing the Jordan River leav-
ing the West Bank. I sit with my six-year-old son at breakfast.
Curious George. I walk a random street in Kolkata surrounded
by a waist-high cloud of street kids. My daughter, fourteen, sings
Rihanna, "Stay," at a local café. The tires hit gravel as I enter a
driveway in an Istrian vineyard with my eighty-three-year-old
father, the owner's arms outstretched to great us. I drive with
my wife to the Graves plantation for a family reunion on the
land where her family was owned. Stones with no names mark

the woods. Eighty mph on the Dan Ryan in Chicago. I'm on pause while my seventeen-year-old son explains a coded message smuggled by Kendrick Lamar into a lyric. I sit with what I can imagine about <u>what</u> the world sees when it looks at me, when it watches me, mine, what the world misses when it doesn't, what I see when I look out, or back. A voice to spill the body into. The violence (always?) inherent in seeing people for what they are. History. Poems might link all that crucial what-business to some version of <u>who</u> sees, who listens, how seen, who reaches out, and who tucks a chin behind a what collar, who ducks around what corner inside themselves.

Interlude: James Scully

At best a poem is not a thing but a practice. A social practice. At the very least it is a social function. But any poem is socially conditioned, constituted and effected insofar as it is produced *by, about, through* and *for.*

*

POETRY: UP AGAINST THE WALL OF THE ELEVENTH THESIS

Marx's Eleventh Thesis on Feuerbach, tweaked by Engels, reads: "Philosophers have hitherto interpreted the world in various ways; the point is to change it." Which implies the philosophers' shortcoming is historical, not fatal. Conceivably they could, like Marx himself, work to change the world.

But what if philosophers were poets? We'd have to eliminate "hitherto," change the tense, and say: "Poets interpret the world; the point is to change it." In the US poetry domain, the suggestion that poets might even *try* to change the world is too absurd for words.

The assumption that poetry may have affect, but not effect, is not confined to the aesthetic of *belles lettres* (fine writing supposedly for its own sake). Surprisingly, much political poetry also presumes its own inefficacy. Even when it's militant. It gives itself away, perhaps being delivered as a cascading wall of words. Or it's fiddled with—as wordy wordplay, say, with ingrown references hardly anyone could follow or absorb. Technically the content may be political, but the body language of the text tells another story. In essence its relationship with its audience is ceremonial: less a communication than a ritual.

I raise this as a caveat—that there are more dimensions to the poetry-&/as-politics question than can be considered here. Much of what goes into poetry is sublimated as a complex of felt presences that don't show up as print: e.g. the body language of the poetry, the class-cued intensity or passivity of the idiom, etc. These also create meaning.

Another caveat. The virtual truism that political, economic or other systemic social realities are out of poetic bounds, or are aesthetically degrading, is historically ignorant. It is contradicted even by the standard canon of Western Civ drama and poetry, as well as poetry throughout the world. Yet the Anglophone literary world, even in avant phases, seems instinctively to keep within a *belles lettres* reservation. As against that there is the Salvadoran poet Roque Dalton, saying: "Whatever fits into life, fits into poetry." Whitman had a similar understanding. Yet here and now any political poetry—meaning poetry that goes against the dominant political grain, or that incorporates supposedly "non-poetical" realities or concerns—is dismissed as "political."

This is no small matter. The highlighting of poetic decorum—of what's "appropriate" to poetry—preempts the question of poetic *efficacy*. Makes it unthinkable. God help whoever breaks that silence, creating an *effect*. Baraka's "Somebody Blew Up America" is a rare instance wherein the breach of poetic (and extra-poetic!) decorum spilled over into the "real world." Baraka had spoken the politically unspeakable. Raised a fact-based question, in a poem of all things! Somebody landed a poem, live, in the historical world. Unable to strip Baraka of the poet laureateship of New Jersey, the guardians of poetry stripped the laureateship from New Jersey itself—an over-the-top warning to career track poets to stay *on* track. No deviation. Nonetheless this object lesson did demonstrate that politicians will take poetry seriously, provided the poetry doesn't mince words but has serious weight, intention and candor behind it.

Not so long ago far worse occurred regularly, in an era when poets challenged oppressive regimes. Think Kim Chi Ha in South Korea, Nazim Hikmet, Soviet dissidents. Or the poets such as Leonel Rugama, Otto Rene Castillo or Roque Dalton, murdered in Central America. [Now recent testimony has it that Neruda was murdered in the hospital where he was being treated.] Meanwhile the self-disarming of poets and poetries—to where effectively they challenge nothing—is a recent development. Most career poets, who represent bourgeois cultural standards, broach political or other systemic issues only on occasion, if at all. Mostly they do so reactively, spontaneously—devoid of systemic context—as moralists having their say. The "say" tends to be feeble, because they have not prepared themselves or their readership for this. What gets lost, in this self-blindsiding, is the historical depth and systemic physicality of the issues or events that they are momentarily presuming to speak out on. Truth is, a poet can't just decide to write a political poem. Lacking systemic awareness, there's little possibility of a poet's committing to, never mind participating in, the subjective *and* objective truths of that reality. This is not a matter of schooling or lack of schooling, but of gravity: the capability of grasping and communicating the specific gravity of "the situation." The problem then is not in poetry as such, but in us. We've demanded too little of ourselves, and are paying for that with moral, social and political inconsequence.

This failing has nothing to do with moral character, intellectual ability, or writing skill. It is the crippling consequence of having embraced and naively internalized an ideological system (euphemized as an "aesthetic") that does not countenance the recognition of systems—particularly not of the ideologized aesthetic that is itself bound seamlessly into the political, social and cultural systems crucial to the maintenance of *this here* grotesquely deformed social order.

Seeing as this situation is obfuscated further by postmodern display writing—skywriting words over and under other words, like the Young Hegelians combating phrases with phrases—it's crucial that we get back to basics.

Basics, of course, aren't simple. Though political poetry *as such* does breach decorum, in most cases we still operate by "no blood no foul" rules. Reactive, occasional political poetry can be simultaneously produced *and* brushed off. . . if it does not trouble the bourgeois cultural apparatus. But when a poetry goes beyond that tolerable indiscretion—beyond a politically themed but passive apprehension of reality, attempting instead to engage and change reality in some way—it sets off alarms. Because even the bare recognition of systemic realities already effects a change in our relationship to the world we live in.

There *are* ways to develop this recognition. Ways specific to poetic production. Poetic praxis, like basic literacy praxis itself, consists in linking words to their realities. It's an antidote to ideological management and control, which must constantly *dissociate* words from realities. [If it were a psychological affliction rather than a political tactic, President Obama's unvarying dissociation of words from realities would qualify as clinical.] Poetry in this regard has something in common with reality-immersed literacy projects. Both move in an indeterminate, historically saturated area where words and realities are in constant struggle to get a grip on one another. This isn't an epistemological issue, simply. In this or any praxis, words are not just words.

As Paolo Freire put it (in *THE POLITICS OF EDUCATION*): "Speaking the word is not a true act if it is not at the same time associated with the right of self-expression *and world-expression* . . . of deciding and choosing and ultimately participating in society's historical process." Wouldn't that be at the core of any full-spectrum political poetry? *Ultimately participating in society's historical process?* This is precisely where, without any thought of justice or injustice, we cross the line between interpreting the world and engaging it, possibly "growing" the world and ourselves along with it.

In *The Natural History of Destruction*, W. G. Sebald speaks of something called "truth"—not a fashionable word in the literary or political worlds, which in general are so dissociated from reality, all one can do with such words is manipulate them. But Sebald, speaking "in the context of total destruction," can't blow off reality or truth. His historically conditioned reasoning tells

him that "the ideal of truth inherent in its entirely unpreten-
tious objectivity . . . proves itself the only legitimate reason for
continuing to produce literature in the face of total destruction.
Conversely, the construction of aesthetic or pseudo-aesthetic
effects from the ruins of an annihilated world is a process depriv-
ing literature of its right to exist." Sebald evokes, here, the para-
sitic aesthetic we call "politically correct." The significance of the
"truth" requirement is not its morality, nor that it is truth (any
truth, including scientific, is historically conditioned) but that
the commitment to truth, in itself, resists conventional aesthet-
icism—i.e. the domination of words by words, forms by forms.

What's more significant, in making aesthetic authenticity
contingent on truth to reality, specifically the reality of "an anni-
hilated world," Sebald doesn't treat "aesthetics," "reality," and
"truth" as utterly distinct categories. On the contrary. To think
about them as such, in a philosophically idealist way, leads to
a dead end. The categories have to be thought *through* where
and as they exist—materially and historically—situated in their
living social context.

There is powerful precedent for the aesthetic value of
"truth-telling," including in lyric poetry. Aharon Shabtai, the
Israeli poet who is also a classicist, reminds us that the ancient
Greeks [called] citizens who care only for their own personal
interests, and who stay out of political life: *idiotes*. . . . People
here [he says] are *idiotai*, not *politai* (citizens in the true sense)
. . . It's conventional wisdom that poems exist for their own sake,
in a sphere apart, which has nothing to do with the making of
arguments [or] political statements. The political is considered
vulgar and unsophisticated. Literature has nothing to do with a
civic ethos. It's a culture of *idiotai*, in which everyone is out for
himself." Yet even lyric poetry has resisted the ethos of its day.
He cites Sappho: "the most beautiful thing in the world is not
battalions of soldiers, or cavalries or a navy, but the person one
loves." In historical context, a stand-up hold-your-ground poem.
She opposes the dominant ethos of her day (heroic, martial,
Spartan) with an erotic ethos. Or there's Archilochos, a Greek
mercenary telling without apology or embarrassment how, in

battle with a barbarian mountaineer, he threw down his shield and ran away—in effect discarding heroic values. Why die a pointless death? Anyway I can buy a new shield, he says, a better one.

The writer Shabtai is equally without self delusion. He sees himself "as one who works in a system. Poetry is no private correspondence. It is done within a system that relates to other systems. Only in this way does poetry have a function and a place within the public domain."

Which brings us back to the Eleventh thesis. It's one thing to describe or interpret the world, but change it? With words?

Carlo Levi, in his post WWII novel *The Watch*, describes how after the war, with the Communist Party in the ascendancy, petty party functionaries betrayed the peasants. From their historically advantageous position, "the [functionaries] possess . . . the ability to transform deeds into words in order to change their meanings into anything they please." In this way "they [were] able to motivate men and events. It [was] the art of the functionaries to transform events into mere words." Levi goes on to describe the verbal judo by which words, puny words, use reality against itself. The NATO war on the former Yugoslavia offers an extraordinary example of how words, separated from historical reality, can change reality in a major way. The director of the global PR firm representing the Croatian and Bosnian Muslim governments bragged to a journalist that his firm had got "Jewish organizations to back historically anti-Semitic entities and movements." In WWII the Croatians as well as the Bosnian Muslims fielded Wehrmacht units, plus a Bosnian Muslim Waffen SS, the Croatian equivalent of which was the Ustashe. In Croatia they ran Jasenovac, the largest concentration camp after Auschwitz. Harff, the PR man, simply presented the Yugoslav civil war as a "holocaust," with Serbs demonized as Nazis. A monumental historical event, the Shoah, was instrumentalized, weaponized, in the service of philosophically *and* historically anti-Semitic persons and organizations who had engaged in the actual Holocaust. *Never* underestimate what words, dissociated from their realities, can do to and with historical reality.

Conversely, poetic words dissociated from *their* realities disarm themselves. They too are enmeshed in a volatile systemic environment. To quote Shabtai: "Within these political and cultural systems a debate is underway, thinking is underway, and a struggle is underway for change and renewal." But then we too are subject to this environment. Poetry that does not register this condition—not as a topic, but as the air we breathe—is at risk of trivializing itself. Ironically, a number of those who write such feckless poetry are active in their lives, but rein themselves in where they should be most active, powerful and effective: in their work as writers, the one context in which they may challenge the apparatus of bourgeois cultural production. Consequently they submit to an aesthetic that has no basis in poetic history or modern international practice. In such cases the contradiction between the life and the work is revealing: it shows how intimately a hegemonic ideology may possess one—here, under the guise of being "an aesthetic."

To recapitulate . . . Most protest poetry is a poetry of denial, unprepared to *deal with* what it is ostensibly dealing with. It doesn't so much challenge hegemonic power as moralize on it, or air its own distress. That's it. However irreproachable the intention, writing of this sort is not innocent. Its body language anticipates its own submission, giving ground to what it denounces or complains of. Not because the poetry is weak, but that it's stuck. Being objectively reactive, it can only accede to the initiatives, and momentum, of hegemonic power in all its social, intellectual, cultural and aesthetic manifestations. Such poetry may or may not take itself seriously, though I believe it does so more often than not, but it categorically does not take its life *in the world* as seriously as in all justice it deserves to be taken.

The opposite of denial, as Marx had it, is negation. The point is not to bemoan a bad thing, but to replace it. Thoreau, who knew the score, made the same distinction when he defended John Brown's attempt to negate slavery, and attacked the mainstream Abolitionists' determination to deny slavery, i.e. to moralize on it. In a speech delivered while Brown was waiting to be hanged, Thoreau, to great effect, used the past tense in speaking of a man who, technically, was still alive. "It was the fact that the tyrant [the slaveholder] must give way to him [Brown], or he to the tyrant, that distinguished him from all the reformers of the day that I know. . . The slave-ship is on her way, crowded with its dying victims: new cargoes are being added in mid-ocean; a small crew of slaveholders, countenanced by a large body of passengers, is smothering four millions under the hatches, and yet the politician asserts that the only proper way by which deliverance is to be obtained, is by 'the quiet diffusion of the sentiments of humanity,' without any 'outbreak.' As if the sentiments of humanity were ever found unaccompanied by its deeds . . What is that that I hear cast overboard? The bodies of the dead that have found deliverance. That is the way we are 'diffusing' humanity, and its sentiments with it."

*

Realistically, in what sense may poetry constitute a praxis, a transformative political act?

Praxis is open-ended, dynamic, thinking/acting/learning activity—learning coming through the contradictions, the cracks opened, between what was thought and what is learned in the application of the thought, followed by the re-self-organizing both of thoughts *and* acts, and so on. Because the action in praxis constantly theorizes itself, praxis cannot help but engage power as mediated by formal and informal social, political, economic and cultural structures.

In his 1934 essay "The Author As Producer," a critical take on the New Objectivity movement, Walter Benjamin discusses what must be done, or not done, to realize a genuine praxis. He describes the negative metamorphosis by which political struggle is aestheticized and turned into an object of comfortable contemplation. *The struggle against misery*, he says, is made over into an article of consumption. It's not enough to have a correct politic. The misery has to be approached with the right attitude, otherwise it will be compounded. Quote: "The bourgeois apparatus of production and publication is capable of assimilating [and] propagating an astonishing amount of revolutionary themes without ever putting into question its own continued existence or that of the class which owns it. . . This remains true so long as it is supplied by hacks, albeit revolutionary hacks."

Against this, Benjamin posits writing that delivers the *gravitas*, and sense of urgency, that may transform readers' and other writers' socio-political reflexes. "*A writer who does not teach other writers teaches no one*," he says. One way to do this is to produce a poetry that sticks in the throat of bourgeois culture—to demonstrate the sheer *human* inadequacy of the ideology that passes as an aesthetic. Not to re-ideologize aesthetics, but to re-situate it in the living, lived-in world in all its dimensions.

For Benjamin, literary praxis is not a matter of telling people what to do or think. Rather, it is to create "*a compelling motive for decision*." To shift not simply the bases of thought, but of preverbal social reflexes as well. "Decision" is the first stage of a purposeful act: the threshold where we go from interpreting the world . . . to going out into that world to change it. Of course the effect of poetry, if any, will not be on the world directly. Its effect, as distinguished from its affect, may be mediated, beginning more modestly and realistically as a thought or feeling that hadn't been quite thought or quite felt before, at least not in this larger, graver, reality-based context. A poetry that steps out makes room. It provides instigation and breathing room for others, including for other poets, to *admit to* thoughts, feelings, and intimations already forming, but which hadn't reached the critical point where all that had been obscurely sensed undergoes a qualitative change, assuming an objective dimension and so becoming, in deed, "a compelling motive for decision." There are no guarantees or roadmaps, not in a world where political &/or poetic diktats are a death sentence on poetry as well as on politics. Paradoxically, in this intrinsically social endeavor, you're on your own. But now you *must* move (starting from where you are, in every sense are, *not* from where you want to be or pretend to be) because there is no still point.

Between

[S]TATES OF AFFAIRS are never unities or totalities but rather "multiplicities" in which have arisen foci of unification or centers of totalization. In such multiplicities what counts are not the terms of the elements but what is in between them or their disparities; and to extract the ideas that a multiplicity "enfolds" is to "unfold" it, tracing the lines of which it is composed.

*

John Rajchman is speaking in this passage of Gilles Deleuze's conception of "the fold," applying it to architecture. I suggest that the application can be extended to poetry as well. (Rajchman would point out that "apply" derives from the Latin *plicare*, to fold.) We can think of poetry as that which implicates us ("implicates," from *plicare*). That which places us, or reveals us as always already placed, within the fold. Poetry not as the folded but as the folding.

Nathanaël

ONTOLOGICALLY SPEAKING, THE self is in seism; it produces an instance of instantiation, a *moment of syncope*. If I stand in the way of it, I make myself substitutive, reiteratively displaceable. A translation of remove.

*

"In the open-air prison which the world is becoming, it is no longer so important to know what depends on what, such is the extent to which everything is one. All phenomena rigidify, become insignias of the absolute rule of that which is." — Theodor Adorno, tr. Samuel Weber and Shierry Weber Nicholsen
"A way of happening, a mouth."—W. H. Auden
Might Poetry [*sic*] offer as a réplique: I bury myself in the part of me that is already buried.

Ann Fisher-Wirth

GLOBAL CLIMATE DISRUPTION continues to wreak havoc in the form of droughts, storms, record-breaking temperatures, and runaway wildfires. The gap between rich and poor continues to widen catastrophically, and billions of people worldwide, victims of environmental injustice, lead lives of quiet or clamorous desperation. And this is only the short list of what's going on. We are living out a colossal failure of heart, will, and imagination.

*

No poet is obliged to write about or from a sense of environmental crisis. But after the recent elections, what I wrote three years ago is truer than ever; anti-environmental legislation is being rammed down the American craw as hard and fast as possible. Activism, art, all the ways in which we may express what Galway Kinnell called "tenderness toward existence"—that, it may be, is what we can offer in opposition. To be—and become—good compost.

C. D. Wright

POETRY IS BOTH made and made available wherever there are leaks in the cultural works. There are any number of leaks, for the monolith is structurally unsound, but you have to keep vigilant for signs of weakness, the coming labefaction, and have a vision to carry you through, however makeshift your circumstances.

*

A Plague of Poets

A question posed to Flannery O'Connor as to whether writing programs stifled writers, drew the famous, tart rejoinder that in her opinion they didn't stifle nearly enough.

Even if, as it is often said, there are too many of us, poets that is, that the field is too crowded (as opposed to too many hedge fund managers or too many pharmaceutical lobbyists or too many fundamentalists), time, rejection, discouragement and the inevitable practicalities and detours (some of them fortuitous), as well as, wasted energy, the slow seepage or sudden shift of interest, premature death, burdensome debt or better offers, usually cure the problem of overpopulation. In other words there are plenty of natural predators.

Mihaela Moscaliuc

POETS OFTEN USE "wrong" languages to exert their right, as bilingual or multilingual and exophonic Americans, to write out of and about experiences that do not fully translate into English or that deal with and/or address their complicated relationship with the English language. Through the use of code switching, multi- or trans-languaging, and fusing, these poets engage in linguistic and cultural practices that transmute and revitalize American poetics.

*

Perhaps American poetics do not need revitalizing, or not the kind that requires grafting. Perhaps a hydrating mask will do, or some mezotherapy, some shots of our own fat to smooth out the wrinkles. Still, as exophones, bilinguals, and transculturals writing out of "insides" located outside the American culture and language, we need to let ourselves employ whatever craft feels truthful.

*

My son offers bread to a begging woman. She pushes it away. Bread bread bread, she grouses. Her response makes sense to me, but my son is baffled.

Some hungers are more translatable than others. We assume we understand the obvious ones, that we recognize the universals, forgetting that hunger often shares the same language with desire, that both belong to worlds so private they are barely intelligible.

When Romanian words clutch and twist my English lines, they make some small impossibility possible.

*

I believe we need to read Adorno's statement in the context of his search for, rather than rejection of, an ethics of poetic response to the Holocaust. He cautions against the aestheticizing of tragedy, as he clarifies, for instance, in "Commitment" (1962): "The aesthetic principle of stylization, and even the solemn prayer of the chorus, make an unthinkable fate appear to have had some meaning; it is transfigured, something of its horror removed." I'm reconciled to being the barbarian who removes some of the horror in order to preserve it at all.

Ranjan Ghosh

AN AESTHETIC IMAGINARY is built inside the borders of a nation, a culture, a society, a tradition or an inheritance, but it disaggregates and reconstructs itself when exposed to the callings and constraints of cross-border epistemic and cultural circulations. Aesthetic imaginaries then are entangled figurations bearing out the promise of "shared realities" and what Toni Morrison calls "shareable imaginative worlds."

*

If a poem cannot be written with one finger, it cannot be written with one mind either. A poem might be written in a gusty inspirational sweep but pleads with leisure and patience when subjected to reading. Chinese poetics argues whether we must forget the snare after the rabbit is caught, get oblivious of the net after the fish is caught, ignore the raft after we have reached the shore, dump the word after we have come to know the meaning. This outstanding paradox is what a poem communicates. If sounds can be heard after everything has gone soundless, one must know a poem is experienced after the poem has been read and the writing done. When you thought you were ashore, composed and sheltered, the raft tugs you to speak again. After completion, begins eloquence.

Ulrikka S. Gernes

I THINK POETRY can offer you a kind of asylum, a kind of protection from all the other languages that are constantly screaming and shouting into our faces. And I think poetry can give us an inner strength, a shield, an ability to hear our own inner voices. In that sense I think one could call poetry a resistance movement since it offers a language which can resist all the "official" languages; the language of commerce, the uncommitted and manipulative language of the politicians, the deafening noise of the advertising language and so forth.

*

Poetry
in any language
is a language
of resistance, resilience, resonance,
that speaks from the core and from the rim,
from inner and from outer space
within the experience
of human
existence.

Convergence

COMPREHENSION: WHOLE AND partial, convergent divergent, consonant dissonant, from all one and from one all.

*

Union. Unity. Integrity. Oneness. Wholeness. If the parable Plato puts into Aristophanes's mouth is right, it is the most urgent, definitive desire of humans. No surprise, then, that (in the unification that is metaphor, in the integration we call form, and so on) poetry, too, pursues it so urgently.

Ishion Hutchinson

[T]HE POET IN a mode of professing inadvertently insults the intelligence and sensibility of his audience, whoever they maybe. If these topics, thus politicized, become the poet's template or singular mode of expression, there is something rabid and insular about that. The creator of his poem, Montale finally reminds us, is the one who works his poem like an object, instinctively accumulating meanings and metaphorical meanings, reconciling the irreconcilable within the poem so as to make it the strongest, surest unrepeatable correlative of his own internal experience.

*

A way of happening, a mouth, is what Auden goes on to say, which is not saying anything *about* poetry, now or then or ever, because it needs no ventriloquist: it is happening, a movement of return to the inviolable Word, contained within a poem, of which inexhaustible things might be said. Poetry arises out of a fear of extinction, I believe, so we experience what survives in situ, a primitive joy in recognizing reality we didn't know we know. The mouth opens, an astonished O, to let out sound and to let in sound—this is why the poetic experience is the most complete, for it fuses the vatic divide.

Clayton Eshleman

POETRY TWISTS TOWARD the unknown and seeks to realize something beyond the poet's initial awareness. What it seeks to know might be described as the unlimited interiority of its initial impetus.

*

Degree writing programs are substituting creative writing for poetry. The first poets facing the incomprehensible division between what would become culture & wilderness, taught themselves how to span it & thus, in such caves as Chauvet & Lascaux, be whole, having become aware of their differences from animals. Our key distinction today may become that of being the first generation to have written at a time in which the origins & the end of poetry became discernable.

Ajuan Maria Mance

AFRICAN AMERICAN WOMEN poets and the figures and circumstances that their poems depicted remained marginalized . . . The subjects, issues, and locations that late-twentieth-century Black women poets treated in their depictions of African American women's lives fell far outside the limits that defined womanhood not only in the popular imagination but also among artistic and academic considerations of womanhood where, based on their historically troubled relationship to ideal womanhood and the pastoral homescape, Black women's poems of testimony and resistance were often tokenized and exoticized as glimpses into "the other womanhood."

*

For me, Auden's claim can only be read as ironic. Coming in the wake of the Harlem Renaissance, whose young, Black poets upended conventional notions of language and form in works that wrote their historically marginalized communities into visibility and voice, Auden's assertion feels more like a provocation—to make a case for poetry's capacity to disrupt, create, and transform; and to remember that it is in this capacity that the work is often at its most innovative, insightful, and exquisite.

For African American writers, poetry has always occupied the simultaneous positions of literary art and instrument of social change. In the US, a nation that remains segregated both socially and economically, Black poems are able to enter spaces—racially exclusive neighborhoods, elite institutions—to which most Black people have either limited access or no access at all. In these settings, poems by Black writers might well be the most intimate communications a non-Black reader can and will ever have with a person of African descent. Such poems introduce Black perspectives and experiences into conversations from which Black people themselves are excluded, effecting what the poet Audre Lorde once called a shift in the "quality of light by which we scrutinize our lives."

Bernard W. Quetchenbach

[T]HE STRUGGLE TO incorporate the inner world of the self into the larger sphere of the self's environment, and the reverse, has been the central theme and project of contemporary poetry . . . Self-conscious nature writers are in the precarious position of reaching across the gap between human and nonhuman nature by recognizing their own participation in the processes they observe, including observation itself, while maintaining an uncompromised belief in the integrity of nature as an independently functioning totality.

*

My concern at that time was that human world-making, if acknowledged by what would now be called ecopoets, would transform all that is nonhuman into, well, just one more human preoccupation. But as the glaciers melt and sea level rises, a nightmare version of "the integrity of nature as an independently functioning totality" is voiced by the likes of James Inhofe, who at least claims to see nature as serenely indifferent. Poets, along with everyone else, will have to accept a degree of entanglement that I'm frankly uncomfortable with. I still think there's something out there that isn't just me, in other words. But poetry is all about entanglement; whether we think of poetry as discovering or inventing connections may not be as important as the connections themselves. Adorno's assertion raises the question of whether poetry can make things not happen. Could poetry have prevented Auschwitz? Could it prevent the sixth extinction? Not by itself, certainly. But Auden is still right to the extent that art didn't make Auschwitz happen by itself either. In any case, it's hard to see how surrendering our best qualities to out worst, even if it were possible, would make us less barbaric.

Jeffrey Wainwright

THE "SPACE AVAILABLE" to poetry in the sense of "media share" may be small, but what might currently be done within that space in terms of the variety of style and discourse has wider possibilities and fewer stipulations than any other of the verbal forms.

*

The strength that poetry now possesses—having absorbed the discursiveness of neo-classicism, the subjectivity of romanticism and the fragmentations of modernism—is the opportunity to combine so many different aspects of experience, knowledge and ways of speaking, and to mix them in a way that is richer, more linguistically—that is to say humanly—diverse than any of the argufying discourses it might feed from. A scrap of Descartes, a child's bedtime memories, geology and evolution (popularly apprehended), a bit of argot and verbal playfulness—any number of things—can coexist here as in no other form outside the literary. Of course we strive to think our way through discrete subjects and to impose on ourselves the appropriate rules of enquiry and contemplation and it is right that we do so. But that effort is part of the whole contingent jostle of our mental states which bear the impression of the language about us. The capacity of the poem to speak something of this mix of the mind is what interests me most, though not, I hope, as an interior monologue, but as part of the exchanges in which we seek for sense. What the poem says may not be true but it will not be a stupid thing to say.

Inexplicable

THE TRUE HAS about it an air of mystery or inexplicability. This mystery is an attribute of the elemental: art of the kind I mean to describe will seem the furthest concentration or reduction or clarification of its substance; it cannot be further refined without being changed in its nature. It is essence, ore, wholly unique, and therefore comparable to nothing. No "it" will have existed before; what will have existed are other instances of like authenticity.

*

Theologians recognize the difficulty: that our cognizing things by genus and species cannot function in regard to God, the wholly singular, who cannot be specified, belonging to no genus. Which leaves the pious only indirection: negative theology and its consanguines.

Poets participate in the same difficulty, and must "tell it slant" because the wholly singular in the world, like the wholly singular above it, will admit no other telling.

Charles Bernstein

IMAGINING LANGUAGE NOT in the service of reality—"noninstrumental," "idled," "split-off"—is a central project for poetry insofar as this allows for writing as the production rather than reproduction or representation of reality. To write as if language were an autonomous realm indeed profits reality, since reality itself is a formulation of the language we as a people construct.

*

To write poetry after the Second War is to accept that barbarism is before us, staring us in the face.

*

I have nothing to say and I am not saying it. I have nothing to not say and I am saying it. I have nothing to not say and I am not saying it.

*

Nothing ties me to the actual. (Nothing tires me as the actual.)

*

Poetry is a metaphor for that which has no likeness. (Nothing has no likeness; in that sense, poetry is like likeness.)

*

Poetry is being possessed by the soul of words that are not yours and making them somebody else's.

*

Poetry is the actual words on the actual page. But the problem is there are no actual words nor actual pages.

*

Never trust a poem with its I's too close together.

Derek Attridge

[T]HE TRULY INVENTIVE artist is someone who is unusually alert to the tensions and fractures in the *doxa* and can exploit these to make the unthinkable thinkable, the unexperienceable experienceable. To read a poem and feel one is entering a new world of thought and feeling, to find oneself laughing at a surprising passage in a novel, to have one's breath taken away by a speech performed on stage—these are experiences of alterity, of the impossible suddenly made possible, of the mind and, sometimes, the body being changed by new configurations, new connections, new possibilities.

*

I am baffled—and delighted—by what I experience when I read a poem that works on me. When I am moved by Donne's lines forbidding mourning, or find myself chuckling by Browning's bitter Spanish monk, or seized by some nameless emotion at Hughes's little Frieda looking at the moon, what is going on? How is it that words written a hundred or a thousand years ago can do this to me? Millions of others have written texts just as wise or just as accurate or just as significant in their depictions of human life, so it is not the content that is the crucial factor; it must be the language. And how can a poem have this effect on me again and again, each time as if for the first time taking me into cognitive and emotional and aesthetic territory I had been excluded from by the daily round? I've tried to theorize these experiences, but they remain puzzling to me. What I am sure of is that as long as language crafted thus into its most intense and moving form can have these effects, poetry remains an indispensable catalyst in the lives of societies.

Philip Brady

LIKE WEEDS CRACKING through asphalt, poetry wells up in the crevices, rupturing the slabs of the everyday to striate speech with song, tradition with resistance, and the visual with the ineffable. Evading definition by club, school, or institution, poetry is a kind of subversion that permits our vagrant selves to surface and blossom.

*

Does poetry have no native means of apprehension? Unlike painting, it cannot be completely appreciated by sight. Unlike music, it is not wholly manifest in sound. In fact, absence is at the heart of poetry. By eluding time and place, it somehow includes the experience of absence. It catalogs everything that happens and does not. Poetry is the thing which is incomplete, and which requires belief in something beyond itself. God? Get real. Poetry requires a belief that within language, and outside of any particular iteration of language, there are possibilities that can never be attended at one time. They have one foot outside. They are beyond. They are what we used to call the muse: not a persona, or a Star Wars Force. Instead, a condition, a state of things. It flickers on the page and in the air. It circumnavigates the dead.

Barbara Maloutas

THE ORIGIN OF narratives is related to time but the origin of stories is a mystery.

*

Mystery by its nature is without time and since without time, it is impossible to make something or anything happen in mystery.

Stories live in poverty, idiosyncrasy and are made visible with a cupped hand, expectant. Stories are particular and necessary to poets and those who take in poems.

Poets and storytellers are at one with the poor and humble. Mystery ceremonies are doorways only.

Poetry finds it difficult to be manipulative, have an agenda in its language. Poems surprise poets and are gifts to which poets are open and by which they are changed and enter into mystery.

Douglas Messerli

INSTEAD OF A concept of a unified being, I much prefer a kind of Babel of existence, a body made up of all sorts of different folk speaking even sometimes contradictory statements. How much richer is this existence to the one-voice mentality! Writers, confuse yourself!, I want to shout. Make life difficult!

*

Poetry can cause many things to happen—or nothing at all! You have to be careful with words. If you joke around too much, a line can even punch you in the face! I've known poems so serious about themselves they died before they even got across the last line. Others bit so sourly into their subjects they poisoned the poet with their own venom! Once I tried to read a poem that cared so little for what it was trying to say if fell off the edge of the page into my lap. Another was in such a rage it forgot to say what it was about to shout out. A drunken poet is apt to tap into the gutter. Yet I prefer all of these to that pure white sheet that tries to beat you to the end before anything gets said.

Brian Henderson

[H]ow we see is what we see: the visions of Plotinus or Eckhart describe light as both what we see and what enables us to do so. With the poet, this light can only be language. With the word, the radical poet's search for transformation and serenity originates. But the word is empty and severed from the world because of the predominance of one of its attributes over any of the others: referentiality. The word in radical poetry aspires to the condition of light, and in order to do so it must dispense with its referential function.

*

Someone wrote that passage quite some time ago; it might have been me, or a replica of me. Luckily light is a thing, and every thing is Tardis-like, bigger on the inside than on the outside, and irreducibly myriad. People can only be among their effects.

I would say poetry opens these thingy myriads in their bewildering entanglements. Debris, the Lacanian remainder, memory, not us, us, folds of *noctiluca scintillans*, things blown through other things, words vectored through and into words, each curving the other's space-time.

Rather than fear and anger, poetry enables the possibility of living in an ethics of fragility.

And my quote might be from Fanny Howe: "Bewilderment as a poetics and an ethics . . . is an enchantment that follows a complete collapse of reference and reconcilability. It cracks open the dialectic and sees myriads all at once."

Listen

... THE PRIORITY OF hearing and listening over speaking and writing does make poetry, whatever else it might or might not be, a mode of *responsibility* ...

*

Even in ordinary life we recognize listening as a skill, an achievement, something that can be done well or poorly. "He/she is a good listener," one might say in praise of a beloved, or a therapist, or a friend.

Poem and poet often are identified as entities that *speak*. We describe both as having a voice. But poem and poet also *listen*, and the quality of the listening may bear on the quality of the work more than the quality of the speaking does.

Good listening ought to be an ideal pursued by both poem and poet.

Robert Hass

THIS IS THE only world we've had and it is an exceedingly violent one . . . Would some better and more powerful act of imagination make the world any better than it has been? Is the world better than it would have been had there been no songs or stories that rebelled against the violence in our natures and mirrored it back to us in a way that might have made us, or some of us, hesitate? There isn't a control for this experiment. We have no way of knowing.

*

Reading the famous remarks by Auden and Adorno—line by Auden, remark by Adorno, I think one might as well say that breathing makes nothing happen or that there can or should be no breathing after Auschwitz. We have inner lives partly in language, a music of consciousness that flows in us and through us. Poetry is very good at representing it. And we need to hear each other. If we only heard the public language of intention and information, we would each be alone on the earth.

Philip Metres

To those of us who consider poetry a medium and a tradition of the imagination of conscience, who see in it a useable past and a vital resource for social change, our work is to liberate what has already been written in books and recirculate it in the social networks where poetry can both inspire and interrogate war resistance and peace activism . . . Poets have a unique role to play in the peace movement, because we can bring our obsessive and nuanced attention to language, its rhetorical possibilities, and its formal limits.

*

Poets are the living archive—door to the past, witness to the present, and repository for the future. The noisy hinge between past and future that reminds us we are opening or closing. And: poetry is not merely a way of beholding the beautiful and telling the truth, but also a mode of listening, a medium of dialogue with ourselves and the others we find ourselves among. And to reimagine what it means "to find oneself among." As C. D. Wright has written, we read and write not only to delight and instruct (or be delighted and instructed), but "to be changed, healed, charged." That sort of social change. That sort of social charge.

Piotr Gwiazda

THERE IS A great deal of intellectual rigor and artistic polemic rooted in the very acts of close observation and careful listening.

*

In his book of prose poems *Kopenhaga* Grzegorz Wróblewski captures the tragicomic nature of the emigrant experience (he moved from Poland to Denmark at the age of twenty-three). But there is much more to this volume, as he documents various aspects of contemporary life through close observation (survey forms, junk mail, tattoos, websites, *Jerry's Deli*, quotations from Trungpa and Foucault, news reports from Kosovo and Congo) and careful listening (academic lectures, radio programs, song lyrics, monologues by friends and strangers, conversations overheard on the bus). Wróblewski is thus as much a solitary émigré at odds with his adopted society as an inquisitive, open-minded anthropologist finding himself in this particular corner of global metropolis. As he himself told me, his book owes more to Bernal Díaz del Castillo's *The True History of the Conquest of New Spain* and Claude Lévi-Strauss's *Tristes Tropiques* than to any other source. At the most profound level, then, *Kopenhaga* can be read as an examination of the ideas of the foreign, the alien, the other—a central topic of our time that poetry, in my view, has scarcely begun to address.

Blas Falconer

[JOHN MURILLO'S POEM "Trouble Man"] begins with "the bone of a question" in the speaker's throat. He has left his lover and is thinking about his father's absence, how his father suffered. Hearing Marvin Gaye from a passing car, he understands that the poem won't answer the question of who his father was or right a wrong. The poem, like the song, like a moan, is the response to the "beat-downs" and the "breaks in life," which are what really measure a man. So, I like to think of the poem as this "bone of a question" uttered, the throat temporarily cleared.

*

If you keep a secret about yourself for much of your life for fear of your life, for fear of rejection, humiliation, and violence, then to speak your truth, even a simple gesture of love, can feel like a revolutionary act, questioning the systems of power that would silence you. And if poetry has the potential to be the most thoughtful speech that one can utter, "the best words in their best order," then amid all the blather and bathos, the poem can distill and magnify the diminished voices of those who might otherwise be erased.

Andrea Witzke Slot

ALTHOUGH STILL RELATIVELY hard to find, and too often over-looked in multi-ethnic, post-colonial, cultural, gender, and even literary studies, dialogic poetry has the potential to incite change in the thought patterns that unwittingly uphold systems of sub-jugation and power by allowing us to see the past and the present in new ways.

*

I genuinely believe that dialogic poetry such as Mullen's, with its innovative use of language and ideological points of view in conflict and conversation, has the ability to effect change. But for that change to happen, poetry needs readers who are willing to listen closely to the words and movement of an entire poem. After all, we can't skim a poem the way we might prose. Auden's poem is a case in point. In fact, to read Auden or Adorno's oft-quoted lines out of context is like stepping into a room, hearing one line of conversation, and then jumping in to talk before that person has finished speaking. Read in full, both texts address how humankind lives in "the prison" of our days, and how poetry might offer healing—that is, if it offers more than what Adorno called "self-satisfied contemplation." Poetry can't be a panacea for the world's woes. But it must be said that poetry today *can* incite new ways of listening, seeing, and acting in the world, and, in turn, move us toward a more understanding, humanitarian society. If we listen closely, we might just find Auden and Adorno are saying the same about their own times.

Michael Dowdy

Tu Fu ARTICULATED better than most the strained relationship between poetry and a society at perpetual war . . . The twenty-first century . . . is more similar to Tu Fu's than not. Though the wide-scale devastation now happens in places other than the United States, those who make war and those who make poetry are still at odds.

*

The war-makers also have a poetics. Unlike ours, theirs is hegemonic. Their poetics—"credit default swaps" and "drone strikes," "illegals" and "efficiencies," "too big to fail" and "enhanced interrogation"—makes things happen. *To us.* It penetrates the skin, its syntax and symbols circulate in the bloodstream. It adheres to the iris, filtering how we see and insuring that we don't. I'm nonetheless quickened by poets such as Daniel Borzutzky, Mark Nowak, Melissa Range, and Ida Stewart, whose wildly different poetics challenge those who would privatize the air we breathe, those who "remove" mountains, "outsource" jobs, "reform" schools, and, by immaculate conception, birth corporate "persons." Perpetual war persists. On human bodies, on ecosystems and species, on the past and possible futures, on language most of all. In these contexts, Joseph Harrington's call for a moratorium on pronouncements about "Poetry" makes sense. And yet Mauricio Kilwein Guevara's line spurs me on: "Poetry is spit and fungus growing underground." Own your home? Fine, the subsurface rights are theirs. Prepare to be fracked, for earthquakes. Meanwhile, poems germinate in the sediment, happenings in search of light.

Mara Scanlon

[W]HAT IS INTERROGATED [by dialogism] . . . is the perva-
sive, central assumption that poetry is fundamentally one of
two things: in lyric poetry, an expression of subjective, personal,
isolated experience, a transcendent and self-sufficient *cri du cœur*;
or, in epic poetry, a normalizing, impersonal, authoritative trea-
tise or record which, guided by its confident cultural mandate,
will not accommodate others' voices and needs.

*

Perhaps I study poetry's possibilities for, and forms of, dialogism
(open, transformative engagement with the other) to stay ahead
of the specter of Adorno's words. Poetry is barbaric in the face of
atrocity if it can only turn inward, if it is so radically private that
it can only be overheard, as we have described the lyric; it is bar-
baric if it proclaims a singular ethical or heroic code, if it claims
or is ceded total authority, as has been true for the epic. These
are poetics of solipsism, closure, and control. I have asked: what
is the poetry devotee to do?* "Read schizophrenically, concealing
the love of rhythm, metaphor, line from the part of the brain
that seeks an ethical encounter with the other through the act
of reading?" Political, activist, public: poetry may be all of these.
They can't be the sole way to be fundamentally ethical. As a com-
munity that doesn't accept poetry's barbarity or irrelevance, we
must think about its lines, no matter how tightly wrought, as a
place of openness and possibility, a perpetual threshold on which

we may encounter the other. And the tremendous beauty of language is not decorative; it enables and creates that encounter.

*Scanlon, Mara. "Ethics and the Lyric: Form, Dialogue, Answerability." *College Literature* 34.1 (Winter 2007): 1–22.

Prayer

A METHOD OF purification: to pray to God, not only in secret as far as men are concerned, but with the thought that God does not exist.

*

A method of orientation: to sing as the Partial to the Whole, to solicit What Cannot Be from Who Does Not Listen.

Yahia Lababidi

THE DREAM, AND nightmare, of all artists is that their creations should come to life.

*

Poetry, now, is how we pray. In these suspicious times, poets are Caedmon and poems hymns. Past the personal, poets sing for those who cannot—registering our awe, making sense of our anguish, and harnessing the inchoate longing of countless souls. Unlike prose, poetry can keep its secrets—deepening our silences, so that we might overhear ourselves. Poetry, also, can restore our sight, helping us to bear better witness to Now and, past that, calmly gaze over the head of our harried times. By lending us this third (metaphysical) eye which collapses distances, poetry can act as a sort of journalism of the soul, reporting on the state of our spiritual life. After all this, too, is what prayer can do: serving as our conscience, and reminding us in times of (personal or political) duress of our essential selves, who we might become: "the better angels of our nature." Thus, poetry reconciles false distinctions between *vita active* and *vita contemplativa*—demonstrating how words are also actions. I pray by admiring a rose, Persian poet Omar Khayyam once said. In contemplating poetry's rose—its inscrutable architecture and scented essence—we're made finer morally, able to conceive of a greater reality.

Carl Phillips

Is IT FAIR to say that all great poetry—the writing of it and the reading of it—is spiritual, inasmuch as it is finally a quest (for truth, clarity of vision) for which vigilance—attention—devotion are required? I think so.

*

I have this memory, which may be off a bit, of Michael Palmer describing the making of art from words as "a sacrament." His point, I think, is that language, if it isn't sacred in and of itself, is not to be taken any more lightly than whatever we may think of as sacred. That gives poetry an urgency, to my mind, and distinguishes it from mere play. Poetry contains all the vicissitudes of what it means to be alive in a given time, and as such is a kind of sacred record. Even when a poem captures individual feeling and thought, it becomes part of the record of a community in time. It helps those to come by telling them what it meant to be alive, once, all the ways it hurt, and the ways it didn't. It gives the future context for how to live beyond us. Each word we put down, then, is an act of generosity, a possible source of rescue, including the rescue that pleasure can give—as can company, when pleasure seems far away.

Robert Kocik

POETS ARE NOT accommodated in our culture. At this point, the burden falls on the producers and not the consumers: poets' lack of consequence is caused by their own complicity in the conditions that create such inconsequence. If phenotype does not become the medium of poetry, we're all doomed.

*

Just as Auden's and Adorno's statements are complimentary to the need for poetry (I imagine a poet incapable of writing poetry of any benefit to others without knowledge of the poem's futility and the conditions that deaden others,) writing is indivisible from the unwritable. All a poet does while not writing, while scorning or abandoning or germinating the poem, or while extending it or carrying out its requisite experience, is indivisible from the poem. The concealed poem is integral to poetry's survival and our fullest expression. Just as the unstruck sound is complimentary to the audible, our speech is cosmogenic. We are the cosmos' aural tradition (indivisible from the inverse). Just as the slightly different temperature fluctuations of the background relic radiation correspond to slightly different densities, these densities correspond to the formative energies of the phonemes our bodies formed around in order to be spoken. I don't know how to make even the slightest word insignificant (except perhaps by blowing away the sense of what it says with the sensation that it, simply, is). Just as this statement is a political economy prayer.

Necessity

IN OUR AGE, the superfluous is easier to produce than the necessary.

*

I need, and I need to. Poetry answers both.

J. Neil C. Garcia

[T]HE "UNNATURALNESS" OF English as a language that pre-
cariously "coexists" in the heady flux of local languages in the
Philippines makes it virtually impossible to be perfectly transpar-
ent to its meanings; it only follows that the poetry written in it
simply resonates the characteristically postcolonial opacity—the
problematic non-convergence—between referent and sign . . .
[A]s practiced by postcolonial fictionists and poets representa-
tional writing in English is all the more (self-)aware of the "ratio-
nalizing" imperative under which it labors . . . [T]hese pressures
enable anglophone "realistic" narration and description to reg-
ister, even more emphatically, the mediating role that language
plays between "life" and "art."

*

I don't think poetry transcends culture; I don't think poetry tran-
scends language; I don't think poetry transcends history. Poetry
beautifully encodes the desire for transcendence. This, for me,
is good enough.

  Knowing what we know and coming from where we come
from, we can no longer endorse the old argument that art tran-
scends materiality. However, while it's true that the last one hun-
dred years of merciless social critique has effectively unmasked
freedom as an illusion, it has not by the same token made the
necessity of this illusion well, less "necessary" in our world. What's
left, after a century of being disabused of the idea that we are free?

The answer is simple: what remains, despite everything, is the desire for freedom. Perhaps poets remain valuable—and irreplace-able—in our world because they are the ones who express—and embody—this necessary longing best.

Fred Moten

PERHAPS ALL WE know is that in the absence of what stands against, in the absence that is the dead and false, a poem is generated. It represents these absences, projecting into the future of their structures and effects from which, it would appear, only a god can save us. But a poem is generated, like a transcendental clue for that in which faith has been lost.

*

To write poetry was barbaric before Auschwitz, too, if one insists upon there being a before and after. Subjects are barbaric things, brutally taking their positions and the positions of others. To write poetry is to distill that violence into conquest's accelerant and residue, its fossil fuel. On the other hand, poetry *does* make nothing happen if we let it—there's an appositional releasement barbarians bring like noise in their peaceful surrounding and generative overrunning of every fortification. Poetry senses, in its militant and erotic gift ecology, that we are not a matter of choice.

Mary Ann Samyn

Isn't it Gaston Bachelard who reminds us that we are the curators of our own images? He does not mean self-image, though that might be relevant, but something more like Stanley Kunitz's "key images." I'd suggest key metaphors might be worth considering, too.

And not only the metaphors that happen within poems but, more important, the ones that occur prior to, or alongside, or beneath poem-writing. The metaphors that help us gain access to the work and to the process of work.

*

Poetry is practical; metaphor arises from need. What happens happens inside, the only place anything can occur. I too sometimes despair. Then, come to my senses. The world is eloquent. Sometimes poetry, also. So, yes, curation is the task at hand. Powerful work, if you can get it. Timely, always, now.

Adam Bradley

Poetry was born in rhythm rather than in words. The first poem might well have been a cry uttered by one of our ancient ancestors long before modern language emerged. As poet and critic Robert Penn Warren once noted, from a groan to a sonnet is a straight line. In its simplest terms, then, a poem is a reproduction of the living tones of speech, regardless of meaning.

*

I'm presently at work on a book that posits pop stars as poets. But what if poets were pop stars? Would they stop to count the syllables in their lines? Would they separate the half from the full rhymes? Would they feel more deeply because of what they know about the subtle workings of sibilance in sound, or would that knowledge prove an impediment?

Despite their obvious differences, poets and pop stars are united in this: they are both masters of the impractical. If everyday people reserve a certain respect for poetry they do so out of reverence for a craft out of phase with the time, like one admires a watchmaker for the mastery required to do small things with great skill. By contrast, people often disparage pop songs as disposable, mere cultural confections. But where do we go when we wish to celebrate, or when we are forced to mourn? So often it is to poetry and, yes, to pop songs—to the very language that at other times might seem aloof or inscrutable, silly or slight.

Pop songs and poetry share this much: though we need neither of them to live, it's hard to live without them.

Stephanie Brown

[O]THER THAN THIS change in the way I write and the way I revise, I can see no connection between poetry and motherhood. To say otherwise would be a lie. There is no connection via language, no oracle at Delphi or Masonic ritual that changes one into a hybrid of *motherpoet*. And if there were, I wouldn't want to know about it. It's hard enough to be a writer and a woman too. Does anyone ask this question of fathers? Of course not. And who cares, anyway? Men writing on fatherhood would be as self-indulgent as men writing on golf.

*

Robert Johnson pulled a string tight between nails on the side of his house so that he could learn to play guitar because he couldn't afford one. Florence Nightingale rebelled against her conventional parents until she could tend to the war wounded. They would be who they were and do what they were driven to do. The driven will find their instruments. To create is to follow that drive. The letters on the double helix find each other and are moved to do so by the spirit—or whatever it is that calls them to each other. Probably the insistent drive to create is held in pairs of clinging amino acids, but I don't know. They must find each other, and will, when creating a person. If you are a poet then you are a poet before whatever other role you play, whatever sex you inhabit or job you take, whatever other writing you write. I write policies and procedures, but that is not part of my drive

157

to write. You will write about what's in front of you, because the drive insists you do so: ironing, or iron-mongering, parsing words or parsnips; murder, maggots, mercury, music, melancholy. An outsider artist writing an epic book for no one to read or the National Book Award winner whose ubiquitous title in placed on night tables in model houses—both write because they follow the insistent plea. Why would you argue?

Vanessa Place

As I've ARGUED before, and will again, in the age of semio-capitalism, where what we trade are signs and signifiers, most precious of which is the fungible unit of the individual—to wit, Facebook, tumblr, mutatis mutandis—the poetic "I" is the gold standard, the essential unit of exchange. Put another way, poets are the unacknowledged hedge fund managers of the world. Poetry pays.

*

We must write for pigs.

Jaswinder Bolina

THOUGH "HIGH" ENGLISH might be born of a culture once dominated by straight white men of privilege, each of us wields our English in ways those men might not have imagined. This is okay. Language, like a hammer, belongs to whoever picks it up to build or demolish.

*

Poetry is inevitable. If the malevolent space lizards absconded tomorrow morning with every self-confessed poet on the planet, some mournful/ironic/gleeful screwball who never before put pen to paper would write a poem about it tomorrow evening.

Poetry is inevitable, so why do we regard it any better than the brick wall?

The poem isn't a greater proof of the human endeavor than that necessary work, but how often do you stop and marvel at the mortar holding up the library? How often do you ponder the place of the mason in the moral order?

The mason doesn't ponder that question, but this is probably because she doesn't expect her occupation to be anybody else's preoccupation. The wall is bigger than the one who builds it.

Poetry is inevitable. After Auschwitz. After Charleston and Ferguson. After the Syrian civil war and every other. If there's barbarism in writing, it isn't in our best intentions. It's in the way we lament our rejection letters more than the bodies dying, the way we want for recognition.

But, the poem isn't any better than the brick. It doesn't belong to you. Better to lay it down. Better then to forget it.

Travis Hedge Coke

POETRY IS EFFICACY in words. The best prose is poetry, the best speeches, the best songs that use words are poetry. They are rooted in poetry and grown in its soil. And that poetry, that inclination, has been arrived at independently by uncountable human beings . . . Poetry isn't a white thing, an Asian thing, an American Indian thing, a modern thing, an ancient thing. When children learn words and try to communicate ideas beyond their immediate grasp by selecting the best words they have, that is poetry.

*

I think I'll stop trying to beat the same beats before they die. For me, the least interesting thing in poetry as it is received today is a composed voice of conviction. I have respect for the poet who masks their self with surety and safe rhythms, myself sometimes included. But, when we know you lie away your neighbors or you only invoke your family that fit the narrative you want to establish, it's too easy for us to see why bandits wear masks as well as superheroes. The best poetry of Gil Scott-Heron was his laughter. We can all quote it, we can all paraphrase, but you can't write a titter twice the way you can say "bird" and "bird" again.

Joni Wallace

WE PERCEIVE THE world in ever-accelerating image streams. Poetry uses the language of perception and finds the ruptures, the cracks where associations and imaginative leaps shine through. Here we live the harder truths and find glimpses of our shared humanity.

As fiction is to storytelling, poetry is to singing. Like singing, it comes from the deep, high, imaginative, sound-based, spiritual, light and dark recesses of human experience. It is unaccounted for, it does not add up to the sum of its parts. Poetry resists intellectualism. As image streams change, poetry must also change. It is by nature the voice of our times.

*

Because language is how we measure existence, distilled language (or even its dismantling) and the careful attention to speaking, listening, and silence required by a poem, is an essential human breath (albeit a breath for nothing). Poetry exists separate from time, separate from thought; these are much like neighboring trees. And there is the poetry tree, singing. As such, it remains vital no matter what darkness, what folly, what deluge, what will. Context, speaker, history, landscape inform the tree. Its song is existence, said Rilke. Vital.

Kristin Palm

I THINK IT is critical that we ask questions like, whose history is being told here? And who has the right to tell it? And, especially if we are speaking from the viewpoint of the dominant culture, what kinds of assumptions are we making? Where are the gaps in our believing, our knowing, our telling? If we're going to tread in this difficult territory, we need to be able to answer these questions. But I do find myself wondering where, in [the poetry] community, is the room for stammering and stuttering? For humility?

*

This weekend, there is a festival in town. There is always a festival in town. This festival celebrates the border between a large, post-industrial city and one of its multi-ethnic enclaves, and features a community cricket match and a psychogeographic stroll. I believe we used to call such endeavors "pick-up games" and "walking." Turning elemental interactions into art projects strikes me as one of the more insidious forms of branding. When a stranger smiles at me on the street or I lie next to my mother as she takes her dying breath, this is not an exhibition. But it is poetic. Does poetry matter? Of course it does, especially in a time when our every last utterance risks being flattened to a hashtag. What must we say about it? Whatever feels necessary. What might we say? Nothing at all.

Time

So THE LIFE of this action of mine is extended in two directions—toward my memory, as regards what I have recited, and toward my expectation, as regards what I am about to recite. But all the time my attention (my "looking at") is present and through it what was future passes on its way to become past.

*

I looked behind me to see what was ahead. I looked ahead to see what was behind.

The present, having no duration, cannot be measured, and neither can anything in it.

Of the three of me—past, present, future—only the present me is real, and the present me is also the only one I cannot see.

And here is poetry: looking behind and looking ahead, refusing to measure or to be measured, looking at once out of my eyes and into them.

Dan Beachy-Quick

To LISTEN TO genius is to let oneself be guided by that voice in the self that is not the self's own. It implies an otherness exactly where we expect to find identity; it speaks within us a rumor to us, that we are least ourselves where we are most ourselves.

*

"Now" is a strange temporal scape in poetry, or so I've come to suspect. As much as "now" pertains to the given social, political, cultural moment in typical usage, poetry digs up within the word some philosophical paradox that speaks to the human condition in vaster ways—"now" being that moment in which each of us most fully exists, and yet, "now" being the very place in which we're denied dwelling. For "now" for us does not sit still. It abandons us. What I'd like to suggest might both be absurd and absurdly simple-minded. I'd like to say poetry offers us within it a *now* we can enter into in no other way. It keeps open within itself, poem by poem, line by line, that fleeting moment of utmost existence in which, by some miraculous Zeno's paradox, the smallest iota of time reveals itself as the field entire. There we encounter an unexpected quality of lyric, of song: not the words of its music, nor even the music itself, but some silence that can be expressed in no other way. The poem tunes the ear to silence, the silence of *now*, which now is most needed.

Rowan Ricardo Phillips

BLACKNESS ENTERS OUR poems as an other, speaking, making with our language something to be better understood. And whether it is to be understood as something new or as simply the same old voice, whether it is the sounds of a new rhyme or just mere repetition is in the balance for us to decide.

*

"Must", "might", and "now" are pivotal words of unshakeable importance in the making of poetry. But they seem impoverished when we use them to talk about poetry. They flatten and become pyrrhic. As though trying to convince a group of people in a bar that their feet are on fire. Poetry is work, hard work, and hard, at times quite lovely, solitude. When we emerge from the dark with a poem of our own or someone else's poem the truth is that its importance as a work of art, as an agent of change, is of greater relation to the translucent past and opaque future. The present to a poet is a midsummer night's dream to wake up from. A poem is a wormhole the size of a word. There is a cosmos inside of it. This is where we begin and end. Anything might be said now about poetry but nothing must be said now about poetry. Anything and nothing can be adverbs or nouns and therefore they can eradicate or conjure. The mind, at its most monochromatic, may attempt to flatten nothing out into pure adverb but the mind, like the fish that sees lure, knows better.

Jane Satterfield

POETIC INSIGHT OFTEN arises from crises of life or craft, out of the invisible script of events that pass unnoticed at first, their influence more obvious in retrospect.

*

When I wrote the lines above years ago, I was thinking back on a time when the collision of private life and public events made me reconsider the purpose of the lyric. Not as ornament or beautiful enclosure, but as charged, magnetic—a space more inclusive of the various roles we play and voices we inhabit, one that might be likened to an urgent and resonant letter, simultaneously "newsy" and timeless. These days we send actual letters less and less often (a fact which makes them ever more welcome), but this is still how I understand and experience poetry's power to document and transform. In the here and now that will quickly become our collective past, poetry does well what it has always done best: commemorate, cajole, console.

Michael Farrell

POETRY—LIKE MOST art—signifies something that resists the concept of "use value." It's the making of culture. Unlike many corporations, poetry networks aren't making a huge effort to destroy the planet. Poetry entails a thinking about thinking that opposes the thinking in order to wield power of both governments and business.

*

I would put the above differently now. I am concerned with the interplay between language and land: the English language and Australian land (or Australia-as-land). This is a conceptual thing, meaning that, while it is an ongoing concern, it is not always my "theme." An indication of this concern is that I read your question as "What must or might be said now about country?". The land makes me; the language makes me. The social makes me, too, but there is more to the social
than other people: there are other animals and the land itself. It is the difference/ground of every encounter. The earth as whole I'm less sure of; culture I'm less sure of (only that the swirl of the West is a kind of figment). I think poetry is something that we keep finding out about. I tend to disagree with just about everyone about it, but that's okay: I will disagree with myself soon enough. The notion of stepping back from the human is to me a calming one, and one that steps away from the twentieth century quotes associated with this project.

Marianne Boruch

I DON'T THINK poets or any artists, really are *in time* at all. The poem, the process of making a poem, is our stay against time, perhaps against history, against what is public and broadly— often emptily—communal and handed to us, against speech even, for all the words in a poem both emerge from, and finally add up to silence, whatever beauty and terror that may mean.

*

I don't know, I don't know is at least an honest mantra. Nevertheless, before that, a few pebbles down this dark well—

— Up against Auden and Adorno, and equally treasured, is the sanity of Dr. Williams: *It is difficult / to get the news from poems / yet men die miserably every day / for lack of what is found there.*

— Inside the writing itself, we poets may be tapping a timeless state (and, thank god, *losing* the self, not finding it). But one of our oldest great subjects *is* time. That, and knowledge, love, grief . . .

— Every despair is new, yet sorrow is ancient, the horrific with us and with us and with us. The world has ended before. Does that trigger hope or hopelessness?

— A small piece by Borges stunned and stopped me when I was young. Cain and Abel sitting around a campfire in the afterlife, Cain asking Abel or it's Abel's question: was it I who killed you, or did you kill me? What happens if poetry starts from there—

Emmy Pérez

THE POETIC LINE of social justice will not be improved until more poets get up from their computers. Poetic line as picket line. Poetic line as hands without weapons. Hands. Want to kiss the hands of our lover before moving elsewhere on the body. Poets as lovers, not only with each other.

*

"Want to kiss the hands of our lover before moving elsewhere on the body" because the lover is the beloved, doesn't suddenly stop like a country.

*

las américas
the globe

*

The line "These are our fucking guns"[1] in Mexico is not "didactic"[2] to me. Studies prove that cussing relieves stress.

*

---

[1] Kamala Platt "These Are Ours"

[2] A favorite word in MFA program workshops

"I take the globe and roll it away: where
On it now is someone like you?"[3]

*

Sometimes the path of conocimiento[4] appears in poems like malachite butterflies, green as grass. And while making love, an oxytocin-high that helps make or adopt babies. Nurses them: more oxytocin.

*

Sometimes the poem needs an afternoon to be without gender.

*

And on days when the legacies of conquest, patriarchy, and empire wound deeper, nothing can wake me, except the crying baby.

*

Then other days, ready to begin again:
"apricot trees exist, apricot trees exist"[5]

---

[3] Sandra McPherson "For Elizabeth Bishop"

[4] Gloria Anzaldúa "now let us shift. . ."

[5] Inger Christensen in translation from *Alphabet*

Refusal

Maintaining public comfort requires that certain bodies "go along with it." To refuse to go along with it, to refuse the place in which you are placed, is to be seen as trouble, as causing discomfort for others.

*

One possibility is that the best answer (or the only answer) to the question of what should be said about poetry is: *nothing*. Which entails the possibility that the best way to contribute to this project is to resist it, to critique it, or to refuse it altogether. No refinement of the question, no accumulation of mutual goodwill eliminates this possibility.

Gene Fendt

[P]OETRY IS A requirement for human life, for mimeses *elicit the passions themselves* and by bringing them up rightly or wrongly shape them, purify them, or muddy them. It is through philosophy and the arts together, then, that we humanize the passions, bringing them so far as *their* own nature allows into the life that we share with the god.

*

Writing about poetry in general rather than specific poems always strikes me as pretentious and it inevitably turns to bombast and void, especially when *auf Deutsch*. But however often the line is quoted free of its context, I still remember where I first encountered Auden's—in his elegy for Yeats. And there it is not a statement of powerlessness or incapacity—perhaps it is not even a statement at all—but it is part of the instantiation of the act of a poem. The poem nothings political involvement, economic utility, scientific measurement, social networking, cultural interrogation, to leave us standing on the bank of the river, now frozen and scoured clear of snow, and inviting us into the long bracing skate of its freedom. *Than which nothing greater can be conceived* by human invention.

Zach Savich

Essay on how when you write and publish a lot of poetry people sometimes ask you to send them poems but more often ask if you'll write an essay, review, statement of poetics, and do you internalize this, coming to feel that the "best thing" you can do for your poetry is to write essays, maybe a memoir, how about a novel. Is a poet appreciated less as a writer of poems than as a conduit to Poetry, or as one who has survived it, for example when performing in a classroom or "craft talk?"

*

Or as Dickinson said: "They shut me up in Prose." Or as I said: "The difference between poetry and prose is prose." Or as I said this other time: "There's this drug that will devastate your own personal liver so you feed it to a horse (prose) and drink the (poetics) urine. The horse does not survive." What I mean stays simple: I perceive people/poets feeling anxious/apologetic about poetry, how to justify it, though it's not one thing, though it's been in most places I'd want to live, what does this say about everything we don't ask to justify itself? So we get susceptible to compensatory justifications. E.g. of "aboutness" that often has less to it than a *New Yorker* article, or apparent "politics" that can replicate popular disregard of the seemingly inapparent, or ideas that seem unassailable (let me be a sail). Or we advocate for lackluster language as though it's more honest. I still prefer the intimate, inchoate, troublesome, rapt. I believe that insisting on THAT—its being a value, or of value—means more than **we** know, as do most facts. Meanwhile, some say birdhouses make nothing happen (except when you are a bird and live there).

Kit Fryatt

AN OPPOSITION BETWEEN poetries of "process" and "product" doesn't get us [far], since almost all poems are both commodities and instances of temporizing rhetoric. Nor does that opposition map neatly onto the modernist/mainstream one: Neomodernists may "set out in determined opposition to the idea of writing as a consumer item," . . . but the close relationship of neomodernist poetry to small-press and limited edition publishing means that innovative poetry often comes packaged as a desirable object; meanwhile the referential relationship between text and world that is a given in much mainstream work alerts us to the temporality of its language.

*

On the principle that it is easier to proceed from the particular to the general and from the concrete to the abstract, I'd say that nothing can be said about poetry without talking about poems themselves. The art is in any case perhaps too various for very many useful generalizations to be made. I don't think we need bother unduly with either Auden or Adorno. Auden's statement both responds to Yeatsian political equivocation with its own brand of elusiveness and makes a statement which is not in itself very controversial: poetry is not a catalyst to "make things happen" so much as it is an intervention in its own right, "a way of happening." Adorno's "Gedicht" is not precisely synonymous with "poetry" as understood by most English speakers anyway;

and he later retracted the statement. To answer your question simply, I think most of what must or might be said about poetry now should be said by and in poems.

Bettina Judd

WRITING IS ATTACHED to the body. This statement is quite a literal for me; it is my Black woman, queer-identified, round-bodied hand that puts pen to paper, to keyboard, and creates whatever I create . . . To say that my writing is attached to my body . . . recognizes the particular mode of thought that does not separate mind from body and spirit to which I closely attend. I don't find any creative freedom in detaching these things. To detach these things because they may constrict my writing also presumes that the rest of my identity is constricted, in itself unfree—even in my imagination.

*

I have taken a while to respond to you. For that I apologize. I have been busy. In addition, between you sending me this request and now, we have had more police murders of Black folks in cities and towns across the country, including one of my hometowns, Baltimore. Just last week, nine Black folks ages ranging from twenty-six to eighty-seven were murdered during Bible study by a white supremacist man who has been treated by the police with kid gloves. In this context, perhaps it is more appropriate to say I was distracted by the rest of my life. Walk with me through this, because I am trying to respond to your question while being distracted, and making sense of the ways one can be distracted.

"Racism was always a con game that sucked all the strength of the victim. It's the red flag that is danced before the head of a bull. Its purpose is only to distract. To keep the bull's mind away from his power and his energy. Keep it focused on anything but his own business. Its hoped for consequence is to define black people as reaction to white presence."—

—Toni Morrison

So let me say this. What those two white men said about poetry ain't none of my never-mind. As in, they are never on my mind. It isn't even about the content of what they said or whether or not it is valuable. I can't even get there yet because I have been asked to respond, once again, to white male presence. This is a wonderful effort you have here—this conversation about poetics and whether or not it matters after death and destruction—whether or not it matters at all. But again I am a Black woman, I live in America. When am I ever *not* facing, running away from death and destruction? Now, if you don't mind I have work to do.

Jerry W. Ward, Jr.

LITERATURE IS NO parasitic language game. It is discourse designed to inform, persuade, incite, reassure, and so forth. Many new black poets wrote with just such aims in mind and with the understanding that they and the acts (poems) they performed had consequences. They regarded their use of language as serious, and it was a serious condition of good faith that the author's "fiction" be commensurate with "fact." So in theory, and in fact, the new black poetry intensified the normal illocutionary forces.

*

Poetry as a sign and a signified event activates something, even if the something is a consciousness of nothing. As a pre-future writer, reader and critic of poetry, I maintain that poetry is a making and using of languages for purposes of entanglement in the scientific understanding of how particles and motions of life are constantly interrelated. Poetry is a unique paradox, liberating and enslaving the desire for nowness and historicity, our penchant for remembering and forgetting.

Sound is the core of poetry; it is the material state with which we struggle to derive meaning (s) from structures and linguistic units that we agree represent content. The less we talk about poetry, the better. Our greatest profit from poetry is living in and learning from a poem.

Eleanor Wilner

THERE IS ANOTHER, , less binary way [than T. S. Eliot's] of think-
ing about the poet's necessary remove, a distancing that permits
vision for which impersonal seems the wrong formulation. In
place of *impersonal*, I would propose *transpersonal*, for it keeps
persons—individually and collectively—in the picture, yet gets
us beyond the merely personal. The word refers to the ability of
our poetic imagination to remove us to the place where we can
join our lives and perceptions with those of others.

*

One-liners, like Auden's and Adorno's, being contentious, cate-
gorical and quotable, hang around seemingly forever, generate
endless all-or-nothing arguments, and fail to encourage thought.

I don't see poetry as a single entity, so can't answer your ques-
tion as it is framed. What I can say is that I have found great
pleasure and meaning in the practice of poetry over a lifetime,
and rejoice in the extraordinary friends this practice has brought
me whom I would never otherwise have known.

Metta Sáma

MINNIE BRUCE PRATT said, "I returned to poetry not because I had 'become a lesbian' but because I had returned to my own body after years of alienation." This sentiment, that poetry is the space one goes to in order to be inside of their own body, strikes me as the point of contact, the point of conversation, the point at which we excise the ornaments of categorizations. Art places us inside of our bodies. Whether we use those bodies to practice the subliminal, the persona, the pointillism, the abstract, the memoir, we enter in our body and engage from within our bodies.

*

I dare say we have never been forced to bow/defer/kowtow to any words of any human creature living or otherwise particularly white male human creatures living or otherwise

I say particularly because what is self-evident is that white men have historically crafted policies laws philosophical truths about themselves in protection of themselves in service of themselves

I say in service of themselves to indicate the ways in which the founding of the United States un-humanized de-humanized women un-humanized de-humanized indigeneous peoples un-humanized de-humanized enslaved Africans

Of course Auden & Adorno are not U. S. citizens and had nothing to do with the founding or direction of the United

States, yet each of them lived in a place and space in which the society supported white men

alone.

In 1939 on the penultimate day of the year in Tennessee my mother was born on the kitchen floor of a white man who her mother cleaned for. By the time my mother entered the Jim Crow South, Cab Calloway had already published the *Hepster's Dictionary.* The man my grandmother worked for blew his top when he saw my mother, a chirper, staining his floor in his righteous dome. My grandmother was nearly fired for not busting her conk, for bringing her employer down. Where was poetry in that moment? That moment was poetry. A pure expression of lyrical intensity of fracture of rhythm and fragmentation the meter was 4/4 4/4 4/4.

Where was Adorno in 1492 when Columbus made first contact with indigenous peoples and set the path for their genocide? Where was Adorno in 1619 when Africans were brought to the Americas?

I, for one, am tired of engaging with white people who look in a mirror to avoid looking into the world.

Urayoán Noel

A STATELESS POETICS is never quite unincorporated, but always *in corps orated*, non-mono-aural, and attuned to the motion-in-possible. Let the state mint its coin, ours is another currency: the writing, the difficult relating.

*

My "unstatement" references Victor Hernández Cruz's poem "Airoplain" (1976), which locates Puerto Rico in "the guava of independence," (dis)locating the island's status/state and celebrating identity in the synaesthetic realm of taste/touch/sight/ syncopated sound:

"They can keep Puerto Rico just give us
the guava of independence depending on no bodies tortures dreams
of the past or future within the present State no State ever of things"

Cruz's " no State ever of / things" evokes Williams (another diasporic Puerto Rican) and his "no ideas but in things" while valuing abstraction as strategic blurring of spacetimes.

I'm interested in how such poetics explore the relational aspect of that *no-thing* poetry makes happen. Poetry knows the limits of meaning: porous spaces (print/performance, oracular/vernacular). Poetic nothing is always something, even (especially?)

in experimental works like Pedro Pietri's book of blank pages
Invisible Poetry (1979) or Edwin Torres's *Yes Thing No Thing*
(2011). Adorno foregrounds the limits of representation, but as
a New-York-based Puerto Rican poet I'm informed by lyric post-
modernist Julia de Burgos (1914–1953), whose poem "Amante"
("Lover") self-reflexively mines the postwar "social void" as a
personal-political revolution:

> "y haré de ti
> por siempre
> un destello de vida
> en la nada social."

> ("and out of you I'll make
> forevermore
> a flash of life
> in the social void.")

Interlude: Margo Tamez

WHAT IS NOT connected to witnessing and disrupting the violence perpetrated upon our communities is oppressing us. Poetry workshops have to get grounded in historicizing instead of ahistoricizing the privileges of the elites. A fifty-thousand dollar graduate degree in creative writing that focuses primarily on "literature" of white writers is another form of white supremacy and white violence against writers of color. Fifty thousand dollars in student loans is a serious chattel and de-capitalizes writers of color . . . [W]e have to seriously challenge the system which reproduces colonial power relationships within that context.

*

Indigenous Poetry and Poetics: Refusing settler logics in the open-air prison

Most Americans refuse to acknowledge or learn history; and this has created a gulf. Adorno said, "Even the most extreme consciousness of doom threatens to degenerate into idle chatter."[6] In 2009, Azfar Hussain gave a rousing poetry reading linking decolonial poetics and politics of refusal and upholding resistance against conformity and the (re)containing of Indigenous and people of color poetry within the silo of Eurocentric, North American, domination. Transgressively refusing against erasure, dispossession, and voicing a commitment to a space

---

[6] Theodor Adorno, *Cultural Criticism and Society*. 1949:

for empowering Indigenous poetry, Hussain's voice and vision challenged me to address how Indigenous peoples are deeply conditioned to conform to settler colonial logics on the issue of "who owes who?" Student loan debt, homelessness, placelessness, namelessness, stolen language, stolen history, and appropriated pasts—all subjected Indigenous poetics to a perpetual indentured "minority" position.

Indigenous poetics—a formation of transgressive and transnational possibility of refusing—firmly opposed to genocidal denial and in solidarity to demand confrontation and accountability—is insurgent and resurgent beyond borders now, more than ever before. Indigenous memory is time-bending, has a "felt," "blood" memory of barbaric impulses and patterns arising from settler colonial utopias. Indigenous memory—of the body violated, emptied, and repeatedly disposed—counters the dominant groups' evasions of truth telling. Engaging contradictions and logics of US genocides—then and now—Indigenous poetics now relates the Indigenous struggle for recognition, historical clarification, and truth. But, to counter Adorno's pessimism, does not insist that the settler society be emptied of bare life—rather, demands that the settler society *embrace* and *account for* a blood-soaked, bitter, shared and eclipsed *inter-relational* history of violence.

There is the monumental debt, outstanding, staring us in the face; So, no, on principle, paying loan debts to the house that organized the massacres, the removals, the separations, the segregation, and the wall—no. That is the logic of emptying. This is in direct relation to life emptied; life out of balance; and life as war which are extensions of the camp. The twenty-first century mega-wall imposed on Ndé peoples' lands (Texas–Mexico, 2006, "Secure Fence Act"), is a blip on the settler society's radar, cluttered by iPhones, credit cards, trendier clothes, and Facebook "likes," i.e. consumer conformity. Ndé poetics in the space of abjection re-members and re-claims the shared history of 1872 (Remolino Massacre); 1910–1916 (La Encantada-El Caloboz forced disappearances and killing fields); 1938 (forced removals along the Lower Rio Grande). Taking Adorno a step further, the

North American settler society must confront the irreparable fail-
ure of the Eurocentric self, citizen, patriot, culture, border, and
Native Other construct. This is the space—a space of deep-time
truth-telling and critical reconciliation—which the majority of
my poetry workshop cohort members, professors, programs—
refused to engage or recognize.[7]

Adorno's dictum, "to write poetry after Auschwitz is barbaric"
was later modified by "perennial suffering has as much right
to expression as the tortured have to scream." Emptying life at
the industrial scale—and its mechanized, conditioned accep-
tance—necessitated, Adorno believed, a major rethinking of
"philosophy, art and the enlightening sciences." But, in the case
of Euro-American mastery of industrial killing at the expense of
Indigenous peoples, can barbarism be distinguished from cul-
ture? The mainstreaming of enlightenment thought and linear
consciousness in the US is deeply disturbing and unsettling.
As Adorno suggested, in the past, this numbness "irrefutably
demonstrated the failure of culture."

By 2011, an Indigenous elder along the gulag wall on the
Texas–Mexico border spoke openly to media, saying the wall
is "an open-air prison." The elder wasn't pointing to the Jewish
Holocaust of which, in south Texas, she had only the state's
version, and had no idea of Adorno; rather, she spoke bluntly
to the Indigenous precedent for the Holocaust—the mass geno-
cides committed against Indigenous peoples in the Texas–Mexico
region, and throughout North America (US, Canada, Mexico)
which underpinned the rise of the modern, settler, military
nation-state.

American fascism is hinged upon continuing domination
over Indigenous peoples, and has persisted . . . through time
. . . as sport, anthem, religion, law . . . converted into total-
izing social amnesia.[8] "Unfree" minds and bodies are assimi-
lated to comfort, that is, what Anna-Verena Nosthoff refers to as
"self-incurred tutelage," the conditioning to need valorization by

---

[7] With a few exceptions, notably, Norman Dubie and Beckian Fritz Goldberg.

[8] Adorno, Theodor W. *Negative Dialectics*. London and New York: Continuum
International Publishing Group. 2005: 358.

dominating groups controlling the power to empty life.[9] Native American/Mexican American—two totalizing identifiers for the homogenized Native Other, molded into two concrete totalities—who exist in the open air prisons which comprise everyday bare life. *Then* and *now.*

Indigenous poetics, born of resilience, revitalization, remembering . . . and intergenerational trauma is enacted and embodied through refusals to the gulag and wall. Dissident poetic practices—beyond the culture-dominated dictum of the poetry workshop, MFA, the manuscript, and "poetry biz" book tours—Indigenous poetics repositions collective consciousness, transformation, action, and relationships. Indigenous poetics stands against the excessive consumerism of a numbed society's denial ("the thinking being [which] properly has no power"[10]). This embodies a potent "game change" of relational, social, spiritual, mental, intuitive, psychic, and physical restructuring.

[9] Anna-Verena Nosthoff. "Barbarism: Notes on the Thought of Theodor W. Adorno." Critical Legal Thinking: Law & the Political. Accessed May 5, 2015, at http://criticallegalthinking.com/2014/10/15/barbarism-notes-thought-theodor-w-adorno/.

[10] Adorno, Theodor W. 1958. "Einführung in die Dialektik." In Nachgelassene Schriften, Abteilung IV: Vorlesungen. Band 2, edited by Christoph Ziermann. Frankfurt am Main: Suhrkamp; 241.

Citizens

INDIVIDUALS CAN BE seen as operators in a market and as citizens in a society. Both descriptions have perspicuity and they reveal important things about people. But they do not reveal the same things about them.

*

Poetry has at least two civic dimensions. A poet is always also a citizen (of a nation state, and of various other polities/communities), with the rights and responsibilities that attend citizenship, and the risks to which citizenship is subject. The writing of poetry does not occur in isolation from, but as part of, this citizenship, just like any other activity. Also, poetry itself takes place within, and as, a socius. Even the seemingly isolated and solitary act of reading or writing a poem in my garret involves and affects others.

Subarno Chattarji

AN OUTLINE OF American political imperatives provides a framework within which the poetry of the [Vietnam] war can be placed. The political context, however, is not a mere placid, historically removed "background." The poetry and the war are closely imbricated, and it is necessary to recognize the contingency, the historical specificity of certain poetic representations . . . The bitterness of war was buttressed by ideological conflict that presumed moral superiority. Within a field of banal political platitudes and righteous violence, where was the space for recollection and love?

*

Auden's declaration is ironic insofar as he writes poetry that impinges on the reader's perception of the world, offer new modes of imagination and thought. Yet Auden is conscious of a poetic desire for making things happen, of impact, of the prophet-poet-shaman speaking truths to the ignorant world—a desire manifested in much poetry dealing with political subjects such as war. War/conflicts draw poets of all hues to express their pain, outrage, helplessness, empathy, and trauma. It is as if poets—of varying talent—are uniquely qualified to speak of war (and the reams of poor war poetry testify to the contrary). Such poets "importune attention," "reduce art to an endless series of momentary and arbitrary 'happenings,' and [. . .] produce in artists and public alike a conformism to the tyranny of the passing moment

192

[. . .]" (*Forewords and Afterwords*, 1973). As with Auden the best poets of our troubled times speak deftly, ironically, quietly creating domains of refusal that are not shrill and articulating belonging that is neither sentimental nor obsessive. Poetry's vitality lies in its expansion of civic spaces, the embodiment of climates of conscience amidst the accidental and the terrible.

Peter Robinson

THE CONTEMPORARY PERIOD, its parameters covering the last approximately sixty years, is one of enormous change in the varieties of spoken and written English, in the accents of authority and power, the vocabularies of technical and technological innovation, the terms for evaluation and appreciation—and poetry in these years has registered and responded, both critically and creatively, to these developments . . . [T]he poetry wars have been fought out so urgently because they have involved in emblematically contested terms the intractable problems that our cultures and societies have had to face and endure.

*

These much-repeated aphoristic remarks of Auden's and Adorno's were never, to my mind, descriptively true. While Auden's tries to find a place for poetry beyond the instrumental, Adorno's sees poetry as unable to extract itself from the most base of instrumentalities. What they have both done is draw attention, in contrasting ways, to poems being actions performed in the world. As such, they are subject to all the considerations applied to any other human action, whether these be truth-conditional, practical, legal, aesthetic or ethical. Being, in their own ways, parts of a vastly complex social process, poems can neither cleanse themselves of association with barbarism, nor can they extract themselves from the things they may be found to have made happen. When we like a poem, we say it works. And so it does.

Cherry Smyth

Is it something about being the other, being taught self-denial and self-hatred that makes queer poets alert to the consequences and cruelty of making someone the despised other? What I am increasingly drawn to in anthologies and collections by queer poets is an ethical poetry, a poetry that tries to inhabit the multiple other, the oppressed other from the painful experience of having been othered. This seems to open the way towards a poetry of compassion and empathy which returns queer to its original anti-discriminatory, fiery and important impulse.

*

When I called my new girlfriend to explain that I was running over half an hour late for the dinner she was cooking, she didn't shout or groan, she simply said, "That's not cool." So I took a fast cab, not a slow train, and was there in under seven minutes. It didn't seem "hip" to use "cool" but her tone was fair and final. It got me thinking about coolness in contemporary poetry and how often what is ironic and defensive to the point of heartlessness is mistaken for "cool." (Even at his most obtuse, John Ashbery is never cold.) Cool is much more than style and aesthetics, much less than stridency and tricks. Art critic Dave Hickey argues that while irony treats us as fellow slaves, cool treats us as fellow citizens. For him, cool is ". . . demonstration without pleading, distinction without discrimination, dissent without violence."[11] Could old "cool" provide a new rubric to think about poetic power and grace? Watching the triumphant Greek left ride the media plump with metaphors of dignity, decency and integrity, and quoting Dylan Thomas, feels like a dream of cool.

[11]   Dave Hickey, *Pirates and Farmers* (London: Ridinghouse, 2013), 99.

Christopher Nealon

[A] POWERFUL STRUCTURE of feeling in American political life
. . . congeals in the idea that it is a betrayal to think against the
system—a betrayal against one's friends, one's community, one's
art . . . Transposed into an academic setting, the idea seems to
be that, in developing a critical analysis of capitalism, the critic
forsakes daily life . . . If one is a critic of poetry, the too-critical
critic loses the ability to perform subtle close readings . . . [I]t is
hard to imagine a more durable twentieth-century victory for the
right than the persistence of this structure of feeling.

*

Like many of us, I think a lot about Adorno's injunction to soli-
darity by way of guilty feeling. But I think that we needn't imag-
ine that the only way to survive morally, inside the long shadow
of war and of the death camps, is to hew as closely as possible to
the experience of guilt. Think of Bertolt Brecht's great poem of
1939, "An die Nachgeborenen [To Those Who Follow In Our
Wake]," which begins with observations that mark out the kind
of "bourgeois coldness" Adorno believed gave tacit approval to
mass murder:

> Truly, I live in dark times!
> An artless word is foolish. A smooth forehead
> Points to insensitivity. He who laughs

Has not yet received
The terrible news.

Brecht, unlike Adorno, imagines that what is needed from
those who survive is not the commitment or the loyalty expressed
by their debt to those who died, but forgiveness from those who
are not yet here—forgiveness sought by those who wish, not that
they had died too, but that they had defeated capital:

You, who shall resurface following the flood
In which we have perished,
Contemplate—
When you speak of our weaknesses,
Also the dark time
That you have escaped.

. . . you, when at last the time comes

That man can aid his fellow man,
Should think upon us
With leniency.

[trans. Scott Horton]

Joseph Harrington

POETRY IS NOT simply a value-neutral, universal taxonomic or analytic category; it is an interpretive cue and an evaluative epithet that shapes uses and judgments of texts. Indeed, poetry is not determined by poems but overdetermines them; accordingly, poets, critics, publishers, and readers have vied for the power to define what poetry "must be"—whether through critical debate, pedagogy, or through the presentation context and distribution of texts.

Bereft of inherent properties, the conversation called poetry instead stages literary ideologies.

*

Let's declare a moratorium on "Poetry." It's the *word*—with its immaterial associations and exclusivities—that's barbaric, especially to writers. "Poetry is a verdict," says Leonard Cohen. *If* you acknowledge the Law of Genre.

"Significant literary work can only come into being in a strict alternation between action and writing . . . in leaflets, brochures, articles, and placards." (Benjamin)

Any literature makes something happen—to writer and reader, if it's working. And it is work, a work: the scientific definition of making-happen. But poetry makes different things happen than does *political organizing*; and poets are wont to substitute the former for the latter. So you're the unacknowledged legislator: now make the cold calls and knock on those doors. George Oppen wrote some of the greatest poems of his day—*after* a career as a union organizer.

Speaking of "presentation context and distribution of texts," here's an idea: go to http://www.globallabourrights.org/—write a poem to the CEO of the latest manufacturer to use sweatshop labor, telling them to stop it. It will shake some action like no poem you've ever seen.

Everything within neoliberal neocolonial corporate globalization is barbaric. What are you going to do about it, poet?

Ego

TRUE PRAYER IS the exorcising of egotism.

*

The Greek tragedians warned against *hubris*. The Christian religious tradition identifies pride as one of the seven deadly sins. Buddhism includes the concept of *anatman*, not-self.

In this matter, the management of ego, poetry harmonizes with these other cultural products and institutions. Insofar as it *teaches* anything at all, poetry teaches me scale: the insignificance and insubstantiality of my self in relation to *what is*, to time and space and order and life and meaning. Poetry puts me in my place. It reminds me that the sense in which I am not is as robust as the sense in which I am, that you are as real as I am, that my world is precious but not *mine*.

Pierre Joris

THE NEWS THAT stays news had to keep traveling, to nomadize from language to language, from era to era, if it wasn't to run the risk of going stale. A dead language is a language we no longer translate from or into.

*

In (f)act, nothing makes poetry happen more than nothing—and everything else does too. Poetry happens. In the middle voice, between the active and the passive, in the great In-Between, in the *entre/antre*, the *barzakh*—is where it is clearest, unencumbered by the deadweight of ego & the lead collar of personal experience.

To write poetry has to be barbaric, because, as Lyn Hejinian says, "it must be foreign to the cultures that produce atrocities," because it has to come from nothing known so far, otherwise it will be apologetic i.e. excusatorily mimetic of what there is, a simple ss (surface-social) reflection, soft sofa for kulchur nap, cover-up alibi for the pseudo-spiritualities of religion and ideology. André Brink, who died yesterday, said: "Under apartheid, poetry was a fundamental element of survival."

This is so because there is no after Auschwitz after Hiroshima after Rwanda after Darfur after Holodomor after Armenia after Yugoslavia after Sabra and Shatila after North America. We are in it, always, always have been, over our heads, there is no outside to this in the anthropocene. And, to quote Jerome Rothenberg "no meaning after Auschwitz / there is only poetry."

Kazim Ali

I FEEL VERY desperate at the moment and desperately committed to poetry of all sorts. The whole world, as we're coming to understand, is quivering in its place. And we have to figure out a way of being human, of relating to each other and staying alive. We have to figure out what society means, what civilization means, and what our relationship is to the natural and even the animal world! These things are of critical importance and will determine our future, and I think language, poetry, and literature are part of that.

*

You say, "poetry makes nothing happen" like it's a *bad* thing. "Nothing" (as Cage taught us, didn't he?) is pretty powerful, pretty important, pretty full, pretty present. So it's vital even if you are talking about "nothing" the way Cage meant it (he thought it meant "*everything*.") though I'm not. I mean "nothing" or "naught" or *haleech*, the way a Sufi might mean it. "Nothing" meaning the absence of ego, the absence of desire, absence of exploitation of others, the denial of their human goodness. Poetry takes the money part (money is the absence of metaphor) out and puts the human part (breath, body and blood) in. Poetry "makes," meaning it engages in the same creative process that god/universe/shakti/shekina did when the whole planet came together. Poetry makes nothing "happen," which means it actualizes that "nothing" into the world. What we call "civilization" anyhow is pretty barbaric. So maybe we need to beard up and figure out the new path. In ancient Gaza did Delilah shave the beard off of Samson to make him not a General of War but human again. With poetry as a blade we might try the same.

Kristen Case

[I]N THE PRAGMATIST epistemology, meaning is generated through the interaction of mind and world—it is *made*. Knowing is not a passive activity, the mere beholding of an object by a perceiving subject, it is a kind of work, a byproduct of active engagement with the world . . . This sense of the epistemological value of work, of knowledge as world building, underlies much of twentieth-century poetry in America.

*

I know less about knowing than I used to know, so I'll stay in the first person here and steer clear of the imperative. I might say that poetry is an approach to who or what exceeds me, to what is not or not yet known, to what is unassimilated or unassimilable, to what William James called (in reference to thought) "the fringe." This is an old idea about poetry: that it is a reaching after some Daphne who won't be caught, that even a reverdie is an elegy. What poetry is for me *now*, in the middle of my life, is a practice of relation characterized by the always-vanishing of the one or ones to whom it relates me. Poetry now is a practice of caring for the not-now, for both the past and the possible. "Barbaric" means *from elsewhere*. "Nothing" sounds like something that might happen in Utopia. "And if we render speech unforseeable," Bachelard asks, "is this not an apprenticeship to freedom?"

John Redmond

AUDEN'S INFLUENCE IS at once deflationary and permissive. At the same time as proposing a less exalted role for poetry, he offers a much wider sense of what poems can be.

*

The quotes from Auden and Adorno are best read as colorful provocations rather than as dry propositions. With different levels of intensity, both highlight a problem for poetry then and now: the continuing overestimation of its public role. My own deflationary sense of poetry's relationship to the public world roughly parallels the kind of deflationary story which Richard Rorty used to tell in relation to contemporary philosophy: for those of us in the (mainly) secular democracies of the "West," our *public* problems are either technical (how to get better mileage on hybrid cars, how to keep Greece in the euro) or else amenable to banal solutions (being decent, exercising justice and tolerance). None of our public problems require recourse to the kinds of ideas which exclusively circulate in poetry or poetry criticism. But thanks to a host of factors — not least the politics and culture of modern universities and the preferences of funding bodies — poets are encouraged to behave as if poetry does "make things happen." Is one likelier to write better poems by having a deflationary sense of poetry's public role? I doubt the case can be proved; but I would like to believe it is so.

Jonathan Farmer

MOST POETS START out in a kind of Eden, one that typically coincides with adolescence. Convinced of the great importance of everything, their own thoughts most of all, they name the world and find it beautiful. But poets eventually grow up, and these days they tend to learn a few lessons along the way—that the most important thing about many of us is the harm our way of living does; that not only is our self-importance suspect, but so is the idea that we have a stable self; and that beauty may be truth but truth is relative.

*

Increasingly, when I hear the word "poetry," I want to scrape away to the raw materials—a sum of poems, taken together, and poems themselves just groups of words one person wrote in the hope that another would hear or read. But words are remarkably, sometimes frustratingly, absorbent—the word "poetry" included—and to imagine these raw materials somehow wrung out or dried up, purified, is to imagine something impossible, even as the imagination of it often makes room for words to take more in.

To write poems or read poems is to participate in "poetry," to inherit and maybe in some way alter all that word has absorbed. Both Auden and Adorno's quotations strike me as attempts to wring a little out of the word, kinds of self-importance that had oversaturated it, at least in their estimations, in the hopes of

then saying—or not saying—something else a little more hon-
estly. The statements have their own self-importance, as does
this statement that I'm writing now. That's one of the lures of
"poetry," I think: the way it adds everything—even our refusals
of its supposed importance—to its weirdly persistent history of
import and importance.

Jonathan Weinert

EVER SINCE WALT Whitman opened his most famous poem with the line "I celebrate myself and I sing myself," American lyric poetry has tended to foreground the personal ego and its desires. Even a poet as apparently self-effacing and opposite in sensibility as Emily Dickinson worries about the subject of selfhood, its ambiguities and uncertainties: "I felt my life with both my hands / To see if it was there—" writes Dickinson in poem 351 . . . Can there be a lyric poetry that enacts the emptying out of the self, the relinquishing of desire?

*

Air Panel

There is not a sound in the whole night, but then at dawn
    a freight train's gray throat opens,
blows a note across the space
    between the damp black tracks it travels west along

and the small boy's bed I wake into.
    My walls show
groups of Revolutionary soldiers, silent, Minutemen and Redcoats
    side by side, rendered in faux

American Primitive. The drummer's two poised sticks
    approach, but never strike,
the oval of the drumhead strapped
    against the placket of his coat.

Through the window's soundless opening I see
    the cedar hedges pale, then stand out
green. The absence of report
    claps louder than a shot,

and the space it opens out in me
    becomes a sort of cranny
I can sometimes disappear into,
    an absence more substantial

than the boy whose name I followed in the way of,
    knowing even then, as I remember now,
that what I am is not
    much more than air

that passes through a window on the first
    warm day of summer—less,
as there are only briefly windows,
    and there is only briefly air.

The opening phrase is from W.S. Merwin's poem "Lights Out,"
The Shadow of Sirius (Copper Canyon, 2008).

Howard Rambsy II

TRANSMUTING AURAL FORMS of expression to words on a page expands views of what constitutes black literary art and at the same time underscores the connections between auditory art forms and print-based compositions. Highlighting the connections between musical and literary forms was especially important for black poets, many of whom preferred to align themselves and their work with African American sonic traditions as opposed to what they perceived as the more restricting conventions of white or Eurocentric literary traditions.

*

I'm not a poet. Yet, I do run this blog, and it's supposed to be about a wide range of things, like culture, black studies, technology, humanities programming, comic books, you name it. But somehow the writing or, if you will, the blogging mostly ends up being about African American poetry. For long stretches of time, I'll produce blog entries on poetry every morning; thus, I'm inclined to go to bed and wake posing some version of the question: "What more can I say that's useful for people about poetry?" Responding to that prompt over the last few years has resulted in more than eight hundred blog entries, featuring analyses, lists of prize winners, book history, news and notes, countless links, timelines, and photographs all showcasing black poets and poetry. The task ahead involves doing even more to figure out and discuss what people view as useful and making sure I include poetry in those conversations.

James Longenbach

POEMS REAWAKEN US to the pleasure of the unintelligibility of the world.

*

Auden's and Adorno's remarks seem to me more true than false; both of them are strategic hyperboles. It is barbaric to write poetry after Auschwitz in the same way that (as Mark Strand once pointed out) it is barbaric to eat lunch after Auschwitz; that we will continue both to eat lunch and to write poems goes without saying, and the point is that, as we do so, we should be mindful of the place of our small achievements. Lunch makes something happen, but not very much. Auden also said that "the political history of the world would have been the same if not a poem had been written, not a picture painted or a bar of music composed," and his point is that it's dangerous to imagine that the world can be saved from mass-murderers by the writing of poems, even though poems can in certain circumstances be extremely gratifying. Compared to these generous remarks by Adorno and Auden, my own remark, that "poems reawaken us to the pleasure of the unintelligibility of the world," now seems to me a little self-congratulatory.

Jeffrey Pethybridge

IF THE POEM is to be "a sad and angry consolation" [Geoffrey Hill] then the poem will always already be an elegy—an elegy albeit removed from the traditional consolations of the genre: the religious consolation which mitigates grief with the thought of the dead in Heaven or its like; or the natural consolation which lessens grief with an image of the dead become one with Nature.

*

It must be abstract; it must change; it must (still) give pleasure; it must be a counter-force—the imagination pressing back against the pressure of reality; it must reckon, be a reckoning; it must be barbaric—how could it not be; it must be sad and angry; it must be an emergency; it must be devoted to emergent occasions, conditions, and persons; it must survive;

it must be a game of time—show the Age its own form and pressure—the nine minutes tracking extinction, the four seconds of falling from bridge to bay, the ordinary work of day, the math in the breath; and a game of timelessness, immortal epic; it must be a disobedience; it must exceed, be excessive—the sublime halt and rupture, now, the extraordinary flower of the I—since the brain is wider than the sky and data both;

it must be a way of happening—of becoming, through the valley of its own saying, the utopia of the poem: and being new, different in being—even if only for the duration of the poem, its clearing, the small utopia of being changed from it, now being in its wake.

Information

JUST AS THE industrial labor process separates off from handicraft, so the form of communication corresponding to this labor process—information—separates off from the form of communication corresponding to the artisanal process of labor, which is storytelling.

*

Which itself split off from poetry, the form of communication corresponding to the proto-labors: hunting and gathering, making fire.

Amaranth Borsuk

[N]ow that augmented reality provides a technology available outside the realm of large institutions (where you had to wear a helmet and enter an immersive location to experience a holographic interaction with language), now that we can access such interfaces through our mobile devices or laptops, this accessibility enables writers to create work for different technological platforms, and to draw on the idioms of those platforms.

*

Poets, like all artists, take each new technology as an opportunity and challenge to expand the boundaries of what they do—whether that means using typewriters to score the page or figuring out how to get thermal receipt printers to dispense poems. My quote above doesn't mean all poets must put on space suits, but is meant to suggest that those who do ought to think about what these new/now technologies offer and what systems they themselves are bound up in (control, hierarchy, access, surveillance). Since it feels to me like poetry is already mediated language, when I mediate it further, through technology, I try to remain conscious of that second level of intervention so that I'm not fooling myself into perceiving it as some greater immediacy. Yes, these virtual and highly embodied interactions with language offer pleasure, surprise, and humor, but they do not do so more effectively than other modes. This is not to say that

I don't still struggle with Adorno's maxim, which informs my book *Handiwork* deeply, but rather that I am constantly struggling with the desire to interact with language, to take it up in my hands, despite its tendency to run right through them.

Katie Peterson

RECENTLY I HEARD an established male poet read from a book of elegies. The poems were beautiful, tense, melancholy, and minimalist, with the smallest margin of sentimentality. It was only days later that I realized that in none of them did the speaker bring anyone medication, a glass of water, or a meal. The poet's concentration was on the elegiac tasks of praise and elevation—that is, on what the poet thinks he's good for.

*

"The falseness of this: that if I could manage the information I could master the experience." —"On The Poems of Heaven," Katie Peterson, www.likestarlings.com/on-the-poems-of-heaven

There's nothing I distrust more than information except people who trust information too much. For a long time, I thought that poetry could be its own technology, slowing us down as so much else wished to speed us up. Lately I want poetry to be an anti-technology, a way of reminding us that the times where we stand at the limits of our knowledge, especially our knowledge of the facts, are those that make us.

The question is often "what is this poem about?" The response is embarrassment.

One wishes to say something about all poems being love poems but then one is immediately embarrassed.

This embarrassment is a holy feeling. You are suddenly in

the presence of something. But the divinity isn't the person who asked you the question with the word "about" in it.

Beauty hates a know-it-all. It assigns no points for that kind of swagger. It has a habit of turning the knowledge you were sure was useless, knowledge you resented, into poetry.

"Thou, mastering me," writes Gerard Manley Hopkins in his wonderful poem about a shipwreck "The Wreck of the Deutschland." He is talking about God; he is talking about experience; he is talking about the poem.

Aaron M. Moe

ZOOPOETICS OPENS A space within the poetic tradition. This space, though, is not exclusively human. Rather it is a sphere where the old lines dividing humans and animals dissolve into fluid borderlands as one species discovers innovative break-throughs in form through an attentiveness toward another species' bodily *poiesis* . . . Animals are not some nicety or some metaphysical convenience in poetry; rather, poetic intelligence is "bound to animals" profoundly, and necessarily so.

*

When *Portia* spiders draw out their prey (another spider), they slap and pluck the prey's web, imitating the ways specific insects flail. Now a moth. Now a fly. Now a gnat. Call it an ambush through material-semiotic innovation. These shapeshiftings emerge (I suggest) from an attentiveness to other insects, and *Portia's* apparent creativity causes us to reconsider conscious-ness, language, and *poiesis* outside primates, pachyderms, and cetaceans. If we see poetry at home in gestures and in any body (human, spider, pig), we burst asunder the one-voice mentality and enrich Babel. The history of poetry—including the per-forming body, the printed page, the bow of a canine, the sudden metamorphosis of a mimic octopus, ASL, totem poles, cyber-texts, the devious pluckings of *Portia* spiders—manifests a col-lective Protean consciousness. Who dares to hold on?

Adam Dickinson

I AM FASCINATED by the prospects of using poetry as an alternative form of engagement with questions traditionally associated with the domain of scientific analysis. The reliance in scientific discourse on images and metaphors (what is the atom if not a metaphor? What is evolution if not a narrative?) is a wonderful enactment of the plurality of resources required to think through fundamental questions of materiality and temporality, and, ultimately, ethics, identity, and community.

*

The strict disciplinary distinction between science and art is a relatively recent cultural phenomenon. Science, in its most technocratic and analytic form, currently dominates conceptions of truth and falsity, driving political and economic agendas. Practiced at their limits, however, poetry and science have much in common: both abductively discern patterns from disparate contexts of knowledge. Poetry does indeed make "nothing happen," in that it provokes a kind of thinking that is outside the parameters of systematic, technocratic interest. Poetry is useless; and it is because of this, operating at the margins of standard conceptions of value, shifting frames and scales of perception, that it is so potentially powerful. As that art form most concerned with the limits of writing, poetry is best positioned to engage with some of the most extreme acts of writing now being perpetrated in the capitalist Anthropocene. Chemicals and anthropogenic pollution

are not only rewriting our climate, but also our metabolism—
what it means to be a human body. My own current poetic
practice (through biomonitoring and microbiome testing on my
body) seeks to respond to this writing, seeks to shift the frames
and scales of what signifies in order to bring such hyperobjects
into focus.

Michael Waters

OUR AMERICAN-ENGLISH language is endlessly inventive, especially when writers use what Whitman called the "blab of the pave," bringing into poems our colloquialisms, slang, vulgarities—those words we wouldn't ordinarily consider as poetic language. The publication of Ginsberg's *Howl* and Lowell's *Life Studies* in the 1950s opened up the possibilities for such words. Before these books, there was merely lip service given to opening up the language; a certain self-censorship persisted. Poetry was associated with higher education. In the latter half of the twentieth century, though, an elasticity of language asserted itself.

*

Susan Sontag's remark that interpretation is the revenge of the intellect upon art meets some resistance in the pronouncements of Auden and Adorno, though it's possible to claim that poetry begins in aerious nothingness until words begin to *happen*, to convey meaning, and that to comprehend Auschwitz requires a language "more primitive, more sensual, more obscene," the kind that Virginia Woolf found necessary to describe illness. And what was Auschwitz but a profound and fathomless human illness? There is nothing that exists beyond words carefully chosen, beyond the capabilities of our still-burgeoning American language, beyond poetry. What might be said *now* about poetry is what might have been said a century ago, that trends, always cyclical, tend to lead us away from the reason for poetry's

existence. It's worthwhile to remember that clarity remains a vir-
tue, that the line has its own integrity, and that the poem requires
a musical surface. It's worthwhile to balance Creeley ("Cruel,
cruel to describe / what there is no reason to describe") with
Oliver ("there is no substitute for vigorous and exact / descrip-
tion"), or Baraka with Bishop, or any poet of consequence with
any other, all the while aspiring to such consequence.

Olivia McCannon

BONNEFOY'S VISION OF the place of grasses feels like reality, is a perception "which possesses the clear unity proper to beings" and "can in no way be confused with the more straightforward unity of representations born of the intellect only." . . . The need to remain connected to such visions, the affirmation of "presence" even as this is threatened by conceptual language, even as meaning slips away, is what brings forth poetry, and its hope.

*

Poetry, at some times, is where madness is kept. At other times, sanity. I believe in a poetry anchored in externals, in other people, and other places, one which makes the effort to speak and understand other languages, and which deals, as a priority, in wholes. The sanity of this poetry knows madness. It listens, looks, touches and tastes life hoping to garner evidence of a truth it can live by, hoping to become whole, and sane.

Memory

A LOSS OF memory is a real loss of those traces that enable individuals to make sense of what is happening to them.

Torture, imprisonment, and isolation are all attempts at breaking the connection with memory.

Writers, artists, musicians, intellectuals, and workers in ideas are the keepers of memory of a community.

*

We share a present life if and only if, and only insofar as, we share past life and envision sharing future life. Thus do memory and hope interconnect. They substantiate us, though each is insubstantial. We are joined to one another by acts of imagination.

Afaa Michael Weaver

[T]HERE IS ONLY one way poets can go truthfully, and that is along the path of the language that is their own. Poets do not exist on their own but rather in a structure.

We journey through the world and inside our lives to the origin of what names us, namely language.

*

Memory works such that if we think backwards from inside a thought to retrieve the thought that preceded it, we may not locate that preceding thought but instead find ourselves immediately confronting the paradox of history. Reaching from the present into the past is, in reality, a fool's errand, even with digital cameras and recorders everywhere, and there is no technology for recording thought as it appears in the mind. This is the space where poetry is born and where it has dominion. Poetry stands to defy the machine.

Paul Woodruff

ABOVE ALL, WISDOM is knowing who you are. You are a human being: you will die someday, and before then you have time to make mistakes, some of them serious . . . This is the wisdom of the tragic poems of ancient Greece, of which Sophocles's *Ajax* is a superb example. The tragic poems remind us again and again of what it is to be human, and of the danger of having ambitions that are superhuman. The refrain of human wisdom in this tradition is *thneta phronein*—think mortal thoughts; don't suppose you could get away with acting like a divine being.

*

Without poetry there would be no poetry. I have written that theater is necessary for human life. So is poetry. The fundamental value of poetry is that it makes words memorable. Without poetry, we would have no cultural memory beyond the invention of writing. Now that we have writing, we must remember that a written word has nowhere near the value of a word inscribed on the spirit. True, most poems, even by famous poets, are worthless, but a few are lifesavers. I am not the only vet who was saved on homecoming by reading the *Odyssey*. And as I age there are lines I cling to for strength, such as "To love that well which thou must leave ere long." And many others which may mean nothing to you but to me are among those beauties that "always must be with us, or we die." So these poems make something happen.

They give new life to my spirit each time they bubble out of my memory. Some of the poems on my worthless list may be life-savers to you, so I do not propose to winnow them out—or even stop reading them. Without poetry there would be no poetry.

Remica L. Bingham

IMAGINING WHAT WASN'T and crafting what was (i.e. writing poems) was always my subtle act of resistance . . . As a child, I believed questioning what was thrust upon us was a small act of resistance; it was almost as revolutionary as finding beauty in what haunted me.

*

Poetry is about reclamation. Sometimes, you are so small and the world is so big, that you have to write your own history and hold onto it. Every time I put pen to page, these days, I am hoping to save myself from forgetting, maybe save others the trouble of lying about what happened later.

Worry haunts me now. With age comes responsibility and the assurance that people are nothing if not hungry and misguided. Today, I'm writing for my children's sake more than for my own, just like my mother worked the nightshift all those years mostly because I was born. Only grace lets poetry put food on a table, fill a classroom with unexpected fervor or make us feel as useful as our mothers in our strained, imperfect art.

This work lets me take back the dead and rile the living. It's what keeps many of us from shouting every minute of the day. It's a calm I'm not granted any place else. Here, in the wild illu-mination of things, I get to tell it as pretty as I think it should be, no matter how ugly or fearful it is.

Kate Cayley

I THINK OF poetry and theatre as quite linked forms. Not in the use of language—plain and sometimes even clumsy speech is essential to a play—but that success is often achieved through sparseness of execution, through cutting away. And they share an eerily similar relationship to time: they are precise expressions of an absolutely present moment, though poetry is reflective for me, and theatre is forward propulsion.

*

I hope it is not facile or sentimental to say that, after the Holocaust, there *must* be poetry, insofar as poetry is memory, record, inner life, something that can stand against the machine and that can recall, with humility and with shame, that the thinking which made the Holocaust possible is not a unique event in history, that we live in the echoes, coming from sometimes unexpected places. In an era in which our compliance can seem total, and so subtle and apparently benign that it is hard to recognize how deeply it runs (almost a compliance of the soul), then maybe poetry (the "maybe" is important) can help to preserve some spirit of non-compliance, of stubborn contrariness, because it is small, modest, individual, and defenseless—against triumphalism and "we," a radical refusal to be part of the shiny modern project. As for Auden, I agree with him. Poetry makes nothing happen. We make far too much happen as it is. But in the same poem Auden also tells the poet "In the prison of his days/Teach the free man how to praise." This seems necessary to me, for poetry at any time, but perhaps most urgent now, or now, again. Poetry might make nothing happen, but it can show a way to praise freedom, and, through praising it, consider what it is.

Nuance

To THINK CLEARLY then about poetry it is necessary to point out that its aims and those of science are not opposed or mutually exclusive; and that only the more complicated, if not finer, tolerances of number, measure and weight that define poetry make it seem imprecise as compared to science, to quick readers of instruments.

*

Finer tolerances. May I achieve finer tolerances. In all the ways one might mean "finer," and all the ways one might mean "tolerance."

Mary Jo Bang

WHEN I ATTEMPT to isolate poetry from the long list of single-minded activities, and make a claim for poetry that will hold true regardless of the myriad forms it takes, I come up with this: poetry rests on the assumption that language is unstable—unstable because while it gestures toward both the material world and the world of interiority, it can never be either—just as the pipe in René Magritte's iconic painting *La trahison des images* (*The Treachery of Images*) will never be a real pipe.

*

Yes, Adorno did say that and who doesn't love a blanket statement, especially when it's provocative? He later said he should not have said that one could no longer write poems after Auschwitz but should instead have asked whether one could go on living after Auschwitz. Later yet, he said that while he didn't want to soften his original statement, it's "in art alone that suffering can find its own voice, consolation, without being immediately betrayed by it." So, his more nuanced position appears to be: after Auschwitz it's barbaric to write poetry and impossible to go on living but poems give voice to suffering, and to give voice to is to be consoled by.

Here's what I would say: the poem is a social space, a language-mirror that reflects back social experience (minimally, a shared language). In the realm of horrific events, poetic mirroring risks being ultimately reductive and therefore trivializing. In contrast to Adorno's statement, I rarely find such poems consoling; I often find them betraying. That said, poems allow poets to perform their thinking by entangling thought with language. For some of us, it's nice, i.e. consoling, to know that others think. Perhaps Auden, that's not nothing.

Lisa M. Steinman

ALTHOUGH BOTH [RAYMOND] Williams and [John] Guillory call into question [T. S.] Eliot's imagination of some ideal list to which the best poets add themselves, both also acknowledge that we read, as Eliot suggests, intertextually and contextually. This fact about reading poses problems for writers who will not, or cannot, easily claim the avenue to literary authority Eliot envisioned. Such writers need to reimagine the texts and contexts within which readers will make sense of their work.

*

One might redefine what "barbaric" means. Originally from the ancient Greek—non-Greek speakers sounded like they said "bar," "bar"—it means "foreign," or "uncivilized," or, at root, "unintelligible speech." In a post-sound-bite world of tweets and censorship, it may be that we need uncivilized speech, that is, speech that operates outside of the larger cultural narratives informing our sense of interiority and of the world. In such a world poetry is barbaric insofar as it can make us slow down and attend to nuance. It may open the possibility of different ways of positioning selves in relation to others or to the world. The barbaric need not be a yawp or even a right good salvo of barks, but it could gesture toward a different economy than what we now call the global economy. It could foster an appreciation of silence. In this case, it may indeed make nothing happen; in any case, it does not use force ("making" something happen), but it might make real the possibility that readers or poets can, if they desire, be agents of change. To redeploy Cavafy in a context he probably could not have anticipated: "What shall become of us without any barbarians?"

Veronica Golos

I BELIEVE AMERICAN poets must be bifocal—must understand paradox, negative capability if you will, and must embrace a more complete comprehension of history. This might result in poetry that is more complex, offers a truer internal deliberation, and a more careful attention to language.

*

Have we "deferred" to Auden's comment, or to Adorno's? We've kept writing. Perhaps we need to look at our history. Could we say, for example, that after what the US did in Abu Ghraib, poetry is barbaric? Though both Adorno's and Auden's lines move me, we need poetry & witnessing more than ever—who else may we rely upon to tell us truth? To help us remember that we re more than butchers, colonialists and terror makers? More than liars? Isn't poetry the oracle of our times? As Erica Hunt says in the *Boston Review* on March 10, 2115, ". . . the space of poetry [is] imperiled on all sides—by a hemorrhaging humanities, a demonstrably shrinking cultural commons daily threatened with extinction, an oblivious, predominantly white discourse running out of excuses for its homogeneity—" Isn't art necessary as air? How could we believe in our humanness, if we didn't have art as well? That art is a defiant, a renouncing of just that barbaric Adorno speaks about.

Walid Bitar

POETRY AND POLITICS are inseparable—impossible to separate the personal from the political or geopolitical . . . What is an "apolitical" poet? One who implicitly promises not to offend or oppose the powerful cliques in his/her society. No poet would take such a promise seriously.

*

Adorno's and Auden's comments are unconvincing. What was barbaric after World War II and Auschwitz—dishonest writing about war and genocide—was barbaric after preceding and succeeding wars and genocides. Did Auden seriously believe that Lorca, Mandelstam and company were condemned because their work made "nothing happen"? In his contribution to the discussion, James Longenbach gives us more Auden: "the political history of the world would have been the same if not a poem had been written, not a picture painted or a bar of music composed." Actually, much of our greatest art, music and literature is also religious or political propaganda; history would have been very different without it. I cannot imagine a history without it; such a history would be inhuman. North American poets are now relatively free to write about power, not for it. Shouldn't waste the opportunity—many writers on the planet live under cutting-edge surveillance, or in brick-and-mortar prisons.

Brenda Hillman

EACH PHRASE IN a poem swirls like confused metal but seeks its own element to make the whole, which has been of necessity the syntactic expression of the sentence being braced by or compromised by the line. Power mechanisms are subverted. There are no nations. In making metaphor, meaning must suffer but it comes back changed—like Osiris, meaning has its body broken to be planted.

*

Since receiving Harvey's thoughtful question, i have wondered whether poetry has expressive limits. Perhaps it does not, if the word "poetry" conveys experience in social, ecological, political & personal ways. Poetry allows people to stretch experience: how is color is experienced by bacteria? what are gradations of human grief? do inert prestigeless minerals have experience? The alchemical syntax essay Harvey quotes was written in the '90s; i had talked with Barbara Guest about abstraction, color & representation. Poetic meanings are fertile when unstable & shredded to be whole.

Poetry is a nearly perfect medium for exploring basic categories of experience including (1) the perceptions of visible & invisible realities, known & unknown natures; (2)) human events taking place in tribes, cultures & economies; (3) the processes of the mind making symbolic, magical objects, & (4) the units of human languages.

Regarding the Auden & Adorno quotes, these writers made their statements in specific contexts. Auden's is from his elegy for Yeats whose politics were different from his. Adorno's is from a difficult essay most people are reluctant to read. Adorno did not mean humans don't need poetry, nor did Auden mean that poetry is useless. They both recognized the virtues of poetry are timeless & accompany our earthly processes despite the violence created by humans. They both knew it is inappropriate to think any art will cure the ills brought on by greed & unjust systems. The fact that poetry cannot bring redemption doesn't mean poetry is pointless; in fact, it provides expressive accompaniment to epic & micro upheavals & revolutions. Art can't do all the work of love, justice & imagination; it is only part but it is at the heart.

Self : World

An encounter with an other effects a transformation of the self from which there is no return.

*

At no project do I work harder or more continuously than at reconciling my "inner" world with the "external" world. I feel alert and happy when the days are long and the sun is bright in summer, gloomy when my world is cold and windy and dark. I feel my mortality when I see fallen leaves. *Everything* is an objective correlative. At no time, then, am I more myself than when reading or writing poetry, that prototypical mediator between interior lives and exterior worlds.

Vandana Khanna

I HAVE LEARNED that drawing upon the stories and myths from my childhood brings me closer not only to the India of my past but also to the America of the present. I don't have to reject one to accept the other. Being an Indian American poet means I don't have to choose. I don't have to reject *dahl* and *roti* for a hamburger, I don't have to know how to tie a sari or practice yoga. I can write in the voices of the past and in the rhythms of today.

*

When I first started writing poetry it was out of a need to keep the old stories alive through words, to keep a connection to a country half a world away that was my "home" but that I couldn't fully picture myself in. Now, poetry has turned into a way for me to look out past my own window, beyond my own life experiences, beyond the borders of any one country. Poetry has become a way to write myself into the world.

Sven Birkerts

I CAN SEE with perfect plainness the arguments that call for literature to serve in some way the concrete business of living and propose for all art an implicit political role. I can even nod my head to many of the premises, the more so if they are advanced one by one by a nonhysterical individual. But persuade my mind as they may, they are powerless against my intuitive conviction, which I seem to have imbibed with mother's milk, that art bears no instructive relation to life in the world.

*

The more deeply we move into mediated living and the more complexly interconnected we become in the virtual sphere, the greater the threat of a dissipation of subjective selfhood. If poetry cannot exert much force in the public sphere, it remains both an emblem and a means of interiority, asking an attention to language that works to restore centeredness. Not "self-centeredness," but rather centeredness in a self which still feels its roots in the larger tribal history.

Jennifer Moxley

THE POEM RESISTS. It resists coming into being. It resists eloquence. It resists transmitting unpleasant or embarrassing knowledge. It resists grammatical constraints. It resists moving away from simple utterance. It resists revision. It resists completion. It resists success. Hopefully, the poet resists as well.

*

As Harvey Hix points out, Auden's and Adorno's statements, out of context, are absurd. They *need* their histories in order to accede to wisdom. They are not blurbs. The same may be said of the "now." In order to understand it, we must understand *when we are*. A challenge I rarely feel equal to. Yet coming across the following, I experience recognition: "[w]e live in an age that, wittingly or not, has declared all-out war on the dark continent of inwardness, silence, and attention, of the self in its wholeness wholly attending" (Robert Pogue Harrison, borrowing words from D. H. Lawrence's poem "Thought"). If we accept this definition of our "age," then we can say about poetry *now* that it *must* work to preserve our "dark continent of inwardness"; poetry, now more than ever, must create increments of thoughtfulness through which the self may silently recognize the outer edges of its soul in the sense record of another's struggle. The poet must resist the noise of the now, lest all of history be turned into blurbs, without context, without wisdom, failing the life-challenge I wrote of in my "fragment": that stubborn movement towards wholeness, of the present, poem, and person.

Camille T. Dungy

THERE ARE ANY number of explanations for the exclusion of black nature poetry from the dominant canon to date, but in its origins and in each of its major renaissances, black poetry in America has recorded perspectives on the natural world as various as black perspectives on the nation. A broader understanding of this country and its poetry is occluded when we overlook or refuse to look carefully at black poets' varied use of landscape, animal life, and ecological poetics.

*

There is no more reason to write poetry today than there is reason to tell the truth, to take care of the earth and those who dwell in and on the earth, or to be generous to other peoples' spirits. We need poetry like we need all the other positive forces this universe can muster. I can't tell you what will happen if we have too much poetry. But I can imagine a world made dimmer by having too little.

Deborah Fleming

THE LITERARY TREATMENT of the landscape of a nation engenders questions about the separation of observer from the observed. Raymond Williams, in *The Country and the City*, emphasizes the idea of separation that he believes is fundamental to romantic pastoralism and to nature writing in general. Moreover, Williams continues, writing about landscape implies observation separate from the land. Just as an observer of landscape must view it from a vantage point removed from the scene in order to appreciate it, the writer about landscape must achieve aesthetic distance from the subject in order to capture its beauty.

*

The best nature writers—for example Robinson Jeffers, Gary Snyder, Mary Oliver—know they are part of what they observe and acknowledge the necessity of belonging to the earth. Inseparable from it, they know that all they know comes from the earth. Literary treatment of landscape is only one way to express their relationship to it.

Reginald Dwayne Betts

THERE ARE PEOPLE broken and breaking in my poems, people healing despite the cauldron of chaos they live in.

My poems are about race in the way their lives are about race. Race is liminal in America. It is both border and veil. Both what you cannot escape and what distorts your vision. Because race is intricate to the American narrative, and not just the African American narrative, but the American narrative, any question of writers writing races is moot. The better question is what do we choose to know, both in life and in print.

*

Enough, I think — to allow us to be wary of where the world is going, of where the world has went, since madness and discontent have always led the word to witness. And the best poems will tell us that there is value in weeping, even if you've been forced to carry a knife between your teeth.

Lynn Melnick

WE NEED ONLY turn on the evening news to encounter the chew-iness with which our culture tackles subjects like violence. Poems (and poets) that exploit traumatic issues for easy emotional pay-off make me angry, because they're grotesque, and because the inauthenticity shows. It's not art that's worth my time. If I want to be momentarily titillated by someone else's trauma, I could turn on a cop show.

*

No, it is not self-evident at all that we should (continue to) defer to Auden and Adorno—in fact I have always thought it would be somewhat barbaric to *stop* writing poetry after Auschwitz and other atrocities. Who better to speak for us than poets? Should we just hand over the analysis of the world to the paid (mostly white and male) talking heads? Instead, I want to defer to Alice Walker, who said "If art doesn't make us better, then what on earth is it for?" I feel we poets have a responsibility to the world we live in to be of some use in making it a better place, because as *people* we have that responsibility and we must use our best skills to make it so. That said, we make the kind of art we make; it doesn't have to be overtly political to be political. Some very quiet poems can have very big impact whereas some lumbering, hammered-home poems do nothing but indulge the poet. But absolutely I believe that poetry and poets can change the world, can make things happen. Look no further than the #BlackPoetsSpeakOut or Undocupoets movements to see that in action. Words matter, and the echo of those words can reverberate far off the page.

Laura-Gray Street

[T]HE ORIGINS of poetry are embedded in the natural world and poetry has traditionally foregrounded nature in a way that drama and fiction have not. But in our contemporary sense of it, eco-poetry isn't just any poetry garnished with birds or trees; it is a kind of paradigm shift. It is the apprehension of real biological selves (as opposed to fantasy selves) inhabiting this planet along with us, a mix of negative capability and empathy expressed with the cadence, imagery, and wit to make it visceral . . .

*

Vultures and poetry are life-sustaining digestive systems.

Sordid and graceful, despised and embedded, prolific and endangered.

Necessary scavengers, scavenges, scavengings—

Janice Gould

NATIVE WOMEN'S LITERARY maps are constructs that symbolically provide direction or describe a known, remembered, imagined, or longed-for terrain. By coming to terms with these inner regions and states of being, we poets offer ways to know ourselves as humans, as Indian people, as people with purpose and heart. Perhaps literary maps are more honest than "real" maps in that their authors claim responsibility for the writing of the "map" . . . The poem that uses the analogy of mapmaking or cartography thus hopes to tell us about new ways of charting a place or event, or about a new place to be mapped.

*

I love maps, charts, cartographic representations of space and time: earth, seas, waterways, maps of stars, calendrical rock art that tracks movements of sun and moon over periods of years. Finding one's way, interpreting legends, assessing distances and the shape of the land, going in the right direction: these things give me great pleasure. I love stories about places—lakes and peaks, valleys, cliffs, riverbanks—and our familial relationship to them. Not all poems inscribe this knowing, but some poems are geographies of longing or connection. "Often I am permitted to return to a meadow," writes Robert Duncan, a place he identifies as "near to the heart." Dorianne Laux's woman driver "could drive up and down the same street/all day . . ./stopping only for a moment to wonder/at the wooden Indian on the corner of

6th and B." Restless, apparently rootless, her driver could keep
going into the hills, "beyond that shadowy nest of red madro-
nes." The store front Indian she notices was once a tree, tied to
the soil. And now the madrones beckon. Forget the hardware
of "civilization." Maps of words allow a return to the meadow.

Sheila Black

IN RECENT YEARS, confessionalism has become a favorite target of a multitude of poetry critics, often employed as a symbol of all that is wrong with poetry . . . Yet the silencing of or scorn for such so-called charged material is often itself a kind of corrective repression. As a few perceptive critics such as Cate Marvin have pointed out, dismay at the confessional is often specifically addressed at the more powerless (women, minorities) who seek to marshal its power.

*

Auden and Adorno's statements seem to me both true and untrue as life itself. Of course, poetry makes nothing happen except in the imagination, but what is more crucial than imagination? As a crippled child, I gained great comfort when I read Spinoza, who said: "I do not attribute to nature either beauty or deformity, order or confusion. Only in relation to our imagination can things be called beautiful or deformed, ordered or confused." Spinoza implies that "to place value" is primarily an imaginative function. This is why poetry can justly be called barbaric and also why we need it. To be able to imagine beyond one's sphere means that any true affirmation of life becomes an act of cruelty. One must affirm not only the "good," but also the "not good"— the puppy gamboling in sunlight and also the dead dog in the parking lot. Keats called this negative capability, "the ability to rest in doubts and uncertainty." He was dying fast and out of that impossibility devised a way of extending or suspending even himself—the ability to see how a thing like art could be at once both alive and dead; to face the grim but in the suspension of what was known—or could be—to forge a slender opening. Words relate to one another as do atoms on the Periodic Table— in obscure but real ways that release energy. I believe this and also that such chemical reactions only occur to the extent that the poet has grappled with the barbaric and oft-disputed real. This is where we are: We have never needed more a poetry grounded in our grim circumstance; yet never more that negative dark star—the space where we suspend to let the pinhole aperture open and take the picture where light blooms. Words. Light. They are not perhaps so different.

Josephine Park

AN AMERICAN HISTORY exclusion and injustice brought
together disparate ethnic groups [under the designation "Asian
American"]; as a result, the expressive products of this unsta-
ble unity are marked by both a converging sense of alienation
within the United States and vastly divergent cultural inheri-
tances. For Asian American poets, an American poetic tradition
steeped in Orientalism applied a distinctly formal pressure on
their work; they carved their verse into a literary terrain overrun
with Oriental fantasies.

*

Poetry makes nothing because to write poetry is barbaric. This
mashup is a strange truth I have learned as a teacher of modern
American poetry—because so much of modern poetry is about
the nothing that is there; because I really do believe in the pri-
mal force of poetry when, with my students, I dive into the
wreck. This is not to claim that Adorno's "barbaric" resonates
with our American yawp, but to consider both the specific con-
ditions of nightmares of history and the peculiar elemental force
of our poetic tradition. (A facile connection, and also irresistible
because facile.)

Josephine Miles in midcentury traced eras in English poetry
into early America to uncover our predilection for a minor
strand of prophetic poetry, a preference for sublimity shaped to
our empty spaces whose ongoing pull I witness semester after

semester in the classroom. I teach poetry because I am suscep-
tible too: reading together, we all feel the wonder of hands that
can grasp and eyes that can dilate. And in a world full of trou-
ble, the barbarism of poetry is homeopathy: an open space for
experience that is real.

Interconnection

A SUSTAINABLE ETHICS for a non-unitary subject proposes an enlarged sense of interconnection between self and others, including non-human or "earth" others, by removing the obstacle of self-centered individualism . . . It is a nomadic eco-philosophy of multiple belongings.

*

The cultural stereotype of the poet (itself a caricature) sustains a misapprehension of poetry. The poet is isolated, this (unreflective and seldom explicitly formulated) position would have it, so poetry is isolating. But how something is made or done need not resemble what it is done for: I work on my dragster very slowly and in solitude, so that I can race it very fast and in front of a large crowd. So with poetry: it may be written at a moment during which the poet is isolated and solitary, but the resulting poem may yet fulfill Martha Nussbaum's call for "empathy and the extension of concern." Even if/when it is written or read or heard in a moment of isolation, insofar as it extends concern it enlarges the writer's or reader's sense of interconnection with others.

Dean Rader

WHAT CONNECTS ORAL, written, and visual gestures is that they rely on language and they intend an audience. They are communicative, communal, and collaborative. They participate in the signifying world of semiotics, especially text and image. For Native cultural texts, blending the lexical and pictorial is critical for Native people because it replicates the doubleness required to negotiate the symbolic meanings of two integrated worlds. This goes for both current everyday realities, as well as for larger historical ones.

*

Poetry is a project the world needs. In order to make this happen, we will have to both evolve and devolve. By this I mean that we need to expand as writers; we have to enlarge the ways poetry connects us to our lives and the world our lives live into. And, as readers, we need to reclaim the reading practices of the past when the gap between poetry and everyday discourse was narrower, closer, more intimate. Ultimately, poetry is a relationship between the reader and the writer, but recently, that relationship has become a long-distance one. We need to be closer. No poem is complete without the reader there to participate in the poetic act. The great Romanian poet Paul Celan once claimed that the poem is a message in a bottle, and a century earlier, Emily Dickinson made a similar observation:

This is my letter to the world
That never wrote to me

The poem is optimistically sent out into the world asking for participation. Poetry is that message in the bottle. It is that attempt to communicate, that entreaty, that prayer. What must be said about poetry is that it is, above all else, a belief in the power of language to connect us to each other and the world. As everything becomes more of everything, we have never needed it more.

Charu Nivedita

THE WORLD IS in chaos. Literature and books are the only factors that can save the world from disaster, I believe. Nothing can replace literature. Tamil Nadu has become philistine because they ignore literature. Just like eyes are the light of the soul, literature is the light of mankind. The Tzarist Russia is an example. A society can identify its wilderness only through the literature. The writer cures the disease of the society. Mankind would have been extinct without literature . . . Without Literature, man becomes an animal.

*

The enlightened ancient poets of Tamil perceived the human body to be a part of cosmos, and the cosmos in the human body. Arguably it is the highest state of consciousness to see yourself as the cosmos and cosmos as you. The enlightened poet can hold conversations with cosmos that are not subject to time and place.

Because we are talking cosmos, these conversations don't need to take place only when the poet wistfully gazes at the starry sky or finds herself tossing in the vastness of oceans. It could happen while listening serenely to music of the forests or travelling in a crowded metro rail.

These colloquies take place through the medium of language—one of the key carriers of civilizations, histories and collective memories. It is language that forges the relationship between the poet and her fellow humans.

The poet is an alchemist who turns her cosmic visions into words employing metaphors in a process not too dissimilar from splitting an atom into countless particles. The disconnect between her and the reader occurs when the latter is unable to fully fathom this fission and fusion.

Fortunate is the reader who can perceive and witness the conversations between the poet and cosmos and she too commences to feel that she's a part of cosmos. She who can feel her body braided with the cosmos can never create an Auschwitz. In every tiny speck of universal dust, she will begin to see herself.

Rachel Hadas

CULTURE IS GIVEN to someone. A work of art presupposes some kind of recipient, even if that person is removed in space and time, faceless, unknown, unimaginable.

*

When I wrote in the late Nineties that culture is given to a recipient who may well be faceless and unknown, I wasn't thinking about the Internet, which has so dramatically facilitated the seeking and finding of poems, any more than I was thinking of falling in love late in life. We often don't know what we need, or even that we are in need, but it can turn out that we've been waiting for precisely this sonnet or stanza, this line or simile. The poem that reaches out and touches us has been launched forth filament by filament, as Whitman writes of his spider, by someone somewhere writing in circumstances and out of urges apparently remote from us. And yet the electric connection can and does happen. As Robert Frost put it a century ago, "Step by step the wonder of unexpected supply keeps growing." However we define poetry, whatever we think its function is, this mysterious generosity, this profound benevolence so easy to overlook or take for granted, still holds.

Lia Purpura

IT WENT VERY fast. It was vaster than any conscious thought. To be of a moment that folds up distance, *finds* no distance between mushroom and *skull*, allows skull from the first—though there was a patch of new mushrooms right there, shining, fat, rampant, creamy, just-sprung. To be part of a mind that flies past the known . . . , to be part of *an order, a whole, a knowledge, that which arranged the rendezvous*: at that tufty spot on my neighbor's grass, with an airy/oceanic sky above, mushroom met skull, the resemblance bloomed and extended me.

*

The italicized quote above (from Wallace Stevens's "Final Soliloquy of the Interior Paramour") is just the sort of metaphysical utterance I whisper to myself under my breath as I walk; the whole poem is an ode to the centrality of the imagination* and an illustration of how, by way of the imagination, we might "collect ourselves/out of all the indifferences into one thing . . ." "Indifferences"—that's the warm beating heart of the poem's thinking for me, what all poems push against (when they're pushing, not feigning exertion), what they counter (when they're not merely tidily arranging), what they're tossing off (when not preoccupied with failure and postures). Proximity, resemblance, presence, likeness—all these ways of seeing oneself in another, another in oneself, all these states of being, are delivered in poems (and in prose that listens) by way of metaphor, that eruption of deep adventurous description. Poems—the philosophical/metaphysical included—are empathy machines. Yesssss- elicitors. Recognition-theaters. I'm not talking "relatable" (that forsaken way of saying "World, you come to me, I'm tired" or "hey, Art, I'll take the usual"—I mean the unnerving, utter rightness of recognizing oneself as multiple, other, strange—and thus, not alone.

*(how little we use the word! out of fashion? disbelieved? come to mean "fake"?)

Jane Hilberry

IN WAYS THAT are so fundamental that they're almost hard to express, poetry . . . is tied to the body. Intuition comes from the body . . .

*

The day before I received this invitation to write about poetry, sixteen people were shot in the Charlie Hebdo offices. Recently Eric Garner, Michael Brown, Dante Parker, Rumain Brison, Tamir Rice and many other unarmed black males have been killed by police. As a poet, what could I say that would make something happen or that would not be barbaric?

Nothing. But a poetry has arisen in response to these episodes of violence, a set of words held up on signs and laid down in our imaginations in the silent photographs of rallies and protests: "Je suis Charlie." "I Can't Breathe." "Hands Up."

These slogans have a searing clarity. Part of what is so powerful about them is the unity they express. "I can't breathe" makes Eric Garner's suffering a collective experience and a collective problem. "Ich bin Charlie" is moving because the holder of the sign, the protestor, is loosening the boundaries of the self in order to speak with/on behalf of others. What would contemporary poetry look like if it were less tied to the legacy of individualism the romantic poets forged?

Can the body's intuition extend to a collective body?

Shira Wolosky

WHILE UNDOUBTEDLY SERVING to keep women the prisoner (called "guardian") of the domestic hearth, modesty served as well to mediate and bridge private and public worlds. Its restrictive sense did not prevent it from becoming . . . an avenue also leading out of the private domestic circle into the broader space of public and published expression. Modesty as a literary *topos* thus stands in complex relation to its social uses. Indeed, it serves as a manner not only of self-effacement but also of self-presentation and self-representation in both social and literary intercourse, which can be exploited to enlarge or intensify self-expression . . .

*

Auden is dead wrong. He is trying to defend poetry from a utilitarian mechanistic world; but in doing so he smothers it. Poetry is participation, today by entering the technological worlds we now inhabit, an energy of address and circulation, which is itself an event and part of events.

Adorno is in ethical shock. Poetry did not save anything, as The Great Tradition of Matthew Arnold had promised it would. The Nazi killers were literate, loved music, had orchestras at Auschwitz. But, as Paul Celan responded to Adorno, poetry must speak. Its power is to give voice and give words that others can take for their own, to make their way in the world, in beauty and in in challenge and in suffering. Poetry is address, from someone to others, across distance, as response to the world each and all inhabits differently and yet in common responsibility.

AnaLouise Keating

[Paula Gunn] Allen, [Gloria] Anzaldúa, and [Audre] Lorde invent differential subjectivities and nondualistic modes of thought that they use to establish points of similarity among readers of diverse backgrounds. Instead of limiting herself to a single-voiced discourse on topics such as sexism or racism, each writer draws from her experience and assumes complex speaking positions enabling her to explore issues crossing ethnic, sexual, national, and economic lines. This flexibility provides an important challenge to readers' generally more stable notions of subjectivity and selfhood.

*

My life testifies to the fact that poetry (and language more generally) can make things happen. Paula Gunn Allen's, Gloria Anzaldúa's, and Audre Lorde's poetry, fiction, and prose changed my life and transformed me. In part, my above statement alludes to this fact. I focused on these authors because their words have had such a profound effect on so many readers. I showcased their words to emphasize their creation of new identities and alternate forms of solidarity. These authors used language to invent complex communities that thrive on multi-faceted commonalities and relational differences. My view *has* changed from the view expressed in the above quotation: It has expanded. Whereas previously I focused on identity/subjectivity and epistemology, I would now add an explicit ontological dimension: Language and material reality can be synonymous. Language does not simply refer to or represent reality; nor does it become reality in some ludic postmodernist way. Language, the physical world, the imaginal, and nonordinary realities are all intimately interwoven; words and images matter and *are* matter; they have causal, material(izing) force. (This force can be many things, including perhaps "barbaric.") As the intentional, hyper-thoughtful use of language, poetry is agentic. It acts, materializing new things.

Mari L'Esperance

THERE'S A CONFLUENCE of elements that occurs under pressure—images and impulses from the unconscious, images and prompts from the conscious life, the body—at a particular time and in a particular way that make the poem possible. Dreams are raw material for poems, but also teach us much about our internal life.

*

"To be hybrid anticipates the future." —Isamu Noguchi, 1942

In a time of tremendous social, political, and environmental upheaval, we can no longer afford a poetry that only talks to itself—that is insular, self feeding, and one-sided in its preoccupations—that does not consider the depth, breadth, and complexity of experience, of the individual and collective psyche, *and across cultures.* We need a poetics of confluence. To imagine and write poetry now, it seems essential that we each work to become conscious of—and integrate—the opposites within ourselves and in the world we inhabit. Our internal world manifests outwardly, for better or worse. The poem works to alchemically facilitate internal, and thereby external, integration and transformation, often in imperceptible ways . . . but those imperceptible shifts gather and accrue. I'd say that's making something happen. In service of human development, of greater consciousness and accountability, I feel, more than ever, that poets and artists must continue to take in, metabolize, and make meaning of the monstrous, of the unthinkable, and not turn away.

Coda

All poetries, all at once.

No before, no after, no outside.

To hear poetry, listen to poetries.

Said sequentially, heard all at once.

The plasticity with which poetry models experience increases the plasticity of experience itself.

Surprise! The familiar.

Disclosure, against closure and enclosure.

To refuse to refuse.

Old words, new worlds; new words, old.

"Poetry" offers an honorific, but does not name a natural kind.

The word "poetry" and what it nods to: both infinitely absorbent.

Good for whom? Good for what?

In poetry's liberty, my liberation.

Futility, poetry's strength, too, not only its weakness.

Speaking outlasts silencing, but silence outlasts speech.

Imagination decays into pretension.

It says what about our society, that no one need justify tennis, but every poet must justify poetry?

No one principle of valuation encloses the whole of poetry. There's no one whole to enclose.

*Inv*ention, yes, but also *con*vention, *prev*ention, *inter*vention.

Asking what poetry *does* misses what poetry *is*. And vice versa.

Delight and teach if you want, but *activate*.

Anything said about poetry is wrong. Including this.

To create new space *for* the civic would enlarge the space *of* the civic.

What poetry does for me depends on what society does to me.

Critique of complex social processes: a complex social process.

We who shun the crowd ourselves compose a crowd.

To register anomaly in language is to resist institutionally concealed consent.

Poetry's importances need not occur at large scale. It is one form of flourishing, to assemble a sentence at a frontier of grammar, or to secure sense from a sentence so assembled.

To pass the test of the cool, test it back.

I make myself most present to myself when I absent myself from myself. And most present to another when I absent myself from myself.

Poetry makes ever real to me my unreality.

The poem returns me to a place I have never been before.

Another poetic paradox: what I dream awakens me.

I could not understand poetry until I understood that it understands me better than I understand it.

Mindfulness, selflessness.

No poetry without attention, no poetry without *care*.

Truth and beauty, red herrings. Poetry pursues something simpler: *care* with words, *care of* words.

Not utopia, but utopian.

In a better world than this one, in which we ourselves were better, we would not need poetry.

Poetry registers our desire for the transcendence it does not achieve.

Poetry releases what it is released by.

Truly spoken, spoken to a need.

I do and do not inhabit a "now." Poetry names that ambiguity, *and* my attempt to resolve it.

The poem cannot remove me to another world, but does change space and time in this one.

Haste, information's ideal: as much information as possible, in as small a unit of time. Poetry prefers patience: the larger the time spent with a poem, the more poetry offers itself.

Hold time to another temporality.

I insist. That's it. I insist.

Fine, all those swallows twittering in the skies, but here are these hogs huffing in the mud, through snouts thick with their own shit.

I laugh without wondering whether I should. I sing without waiting for someone to listen.

Poetry centers me in an orbital world, entangles me in a rhizomatic one.

More philosophical: *history* can't transform event into wisdom.

Our responsibilities as poets are limitless, because so are our responsibilities as persons.

To see my life as like yours, and yours as like mine: a flawed mutuality, but a mutuality.

Why do we esteem carnivores so, we scavengers?

Why am I confined in here? Why is the world projected upside-down? How can so much light enter through such a tiny aperture?

Excess meaning found, excess meaning made.

Incompletion directs the poem; indirection completes it.

Made not of words and images but of making itself.

So accustomed have we grown to lighted interior spaces that we stop noticing the light is *made* rather than given. So badly do we want "interior light" that we forget it, too, is made.

Will speaking *of* my other enable me to speak *with* my other?

Because we *do* share a language, we *can* share what is not susceptible to sharing: perceptions, thoughts, feelings. Poetry just is the possibility of impossible communion.

One *kind* of secret: a not saying of what must be said.

Others' power imposes secrecy. Tell it slant, and to yourself.

She sang, and conversation stopped. She didn't sing, and conversation never started.

Demos, on condition of dialogue.

If I could listen, we could change.

The first human to paint a mammoth or a horse on a cave wall was the first to represent her- or himself. Except for the one who was already singing.

What the poem has joined together, let no force put asunder.

Until the poem magnified it, I couldn't see how grainy it is, this surface I thought was smooth.

Give me to see more *of* what I see, not more *than* what I see.

As falling leaves reveal an autumn wind, as iron filings a magnetic field.

To *have* form, to *be* form, to *in*form. Each describes poetry, none exhaustively.

Form, to repair irreparable deformation.

Still a name on the stone, even worn away. Still a marker, that stone, even grown over.

I don't have to want decay to recognize its beauty.

From soil, to soil. Me, and poetry.

The poem of the earth would be *of earth*.

Mystery is mysterious not because it withholds, but for what it gives. Poetry is poetic not because it makes, but for what it has absorbed.

Unless mystery inflects the ceremony, ceremony detects no mystery.

"It is a *task* to come to see the world as it is," and a *task* to come to *recognize* another as she/he is.

What calls itself "connection" connects me how, and to whom?

A vision for poetry: universal, equal distribution of the right and the means of address.

A vision for poetry: relentless search for all available forms of solidarity.

A sacred record, sacred for what it records *and* how it does the recording.

Poetry as prayer, prayer as poetry. How speak to WHAT IS except by poetry? How speak poetically except by addressing WHAT IS?

In prayer, I call *upon* what I call *for*, and I call for what I call *upon*. So too in poetry.

No one is watching. A circumstantial fact about poetry at this historical moment, but more importantly an ideal: replacement of shame-based ethical decision principles (I might get caught) with craft-based principles (this would contribute to the integrity of a whole).

Limited by my senses, but not limited to them.

This microclimate hosts orchids and insects all its own.

Poetry cannot stop what cannot be stopped, but can change what can be changed.

The *ceremoniality* of words.

Renewed words renew.

Make it make new.

Language passes through me, I pass through language. I speak, I am spoken.

A name to appropriate for poetry: "catalytic converter."

There's a *reason* we have no word like "bedomestication" to oppose to "bewilderment."

The black market in which I want to exchange: an economy of nuance.

Nuance as resistance: against the reductions of a structurally violent global economy and hypermilitarized global polis, any nuanced understanding or locution is egregious.

Commodification's total victory (where everything is a commodity, nothing is poetry) only intensifies poetry's charge to prove that nothing is *not* poetry.

No wonder there is no profit in poetry. In capitalism, I own only what I exclude you from; in poetry, only what I include you in.

Which logic will stand in the path of market logic, holding grocery bags, but unwavering before the line of tanks?

If it's *my* poetry, it isn't poetry. If it belongs to me, not I to it, we both of us are lost.

Where hope and hopelessness converge, poetry distinguishes them. Where they diverge, poetry elides them.

The poetics illuminates the poetry, and the poetry the poetics.

To bear witness to witness already borne.

What witness we needed then we need so much the more now, *because* so few recognize the need.

To take in the historical context of a poem, so as not to be taken in by my own historical context.

Poetry that serves memory is served by it.

Poetry comes of poetry. Sister to Unmoved Mover is the Unmade Maker.

Whether it was taken away by others or left of its own accord, one's past can be reclaimed. *Poetry* is the name we assign that act of reclamation.

Poetry, itself disembodied, embodies me.

Philosophers speak of the clinamen, the swerve. Poetry invites swerving, and itself swerves.

As new technologies redefine the means for gain (access to new markets, control over information, and so on), poetry applies the new technologies to redefine gain.

What hides *behind* the poem, not *in* the poem.

The settled settles; the provisional provides.

Patter, become pattern.

How aspire to *cosmos* except through *logos*?

Does pattern matter? Apparently. Inherently.

Pattern reveals pattern, and absence of pattern, and disruption of pattern.

My hunger matches no other hunger, but has affinities with every other. Naming the hungers secures the affinities.

We live not among voices but among echoes of voices, and speak not with voices but with echoes.

What I see, I see with wonder. By whom I am seen, I plead to be seen with leniency.

Already my poems no longer exist. Already the chokecherry outside my window has outlasted them.

Words imagine for us what we cannot imagine for ourselves. We who attend words must imagine for our society what it fears to imagine for itself.

To envision freedom: not to glimpse Freedom but to identify inequities in the distribution of freedom; to recognize those on whom unfreedoms are most harshly imposed; to teach oneself to utter, and to hear, words that align their speakers and listeners otherwise, that do not abide the current ways of distributing freedom.

Not inert. Not, when inert.

The larger my conception of song, the more I hear as song. The more I hear as song, the larger my conception of song.

One who really *looks* will be closely watched.

Naming the policing *violence* will not make it stop, will not protect those most violently policed. But the naming might still be an urgent need.

Language to make me pause and consider, language to offer me solace. But also language to turn my stomach, set my teeth on edge, make my gorge rise.

Ecology urges me to seek *in*consequence in life (to disturb/exploit/use up as little as possible). Maybe I should want my writing also to be inconsequential.

A public language to defend privacy.

Measure with numbers for one result, with words for another.

Not all of us have yet become collateral damage, but we all have been collaterally damaged.

Here is what I no longer need. Here is what I never needed.

Who are the meaning photosynthesizers? The meaning predators? The meaning scavengers?

Poetry's centripetal force pulls me ever farther from any center. Is there a counterforce to keep me from simply falling away?

What cannot be understood otherwise than otherwise.

Transformed *how*? Into *what*?

The whole contingent of the contingent, contingently.

Self-possession, and the audacity to challenge it.

True, poetry can do nothing by itself, but it does not exist by itself.

That double image—life, and the experience of life—is the feature we humans claim as unique to our vision, and that we poets claim as unique to *our* vision.

Never mind the poem's meaning. Give me its *texture*, what enters through my fingers, my skin.

Never to close the open question.

Nothing changes poetry, poetry changes nothing. But things change, poetry changes, and always the question is whether we ourselves can.

Poetry, because there are no instructions for *how* to revise your life.

Yes, let's chat about something other than death, as soon as I'm no longer facing it.

The mad regard madness and sanity as one; the sane, as two. Who can adjudicate between them?

The simplicity of the complex replaces the complexity of the simple, and is replaced by it.

Attentiveness to language, a second-order attentiveness to the world, incites a first-order attentiveness.

Poetry is to experience as a name to a person.

I trust nothing I have said about poetry, but I trust that distrust.

Of course no one will remember me after I am gone. How could they, when I cannot remember myself now, and was never here?

Works Cited

Introduction

Wendy Brown, *Undoing the Demos: Neoliberalism's Stealth Revolution* (Zone Books, 2015), 9, 10, 202–3.

James P. Carse, *Finite and Infinite Games: A Vision of Life as Play and Possibility* (Free Press, 1986), 8–9.

Bonnie Costello, *Planets on Tables: Poetry, Still Life, and the Turning World* (Cornell Univ. Press, 2008), xiv.

Václav Havel, *Open Letters: Selected Writings, 1965–1990* (Vintage, 1992), 389.

Christian Moraru, *Cosmodernism: American Narrative, Late Globalization, and the New Cultural Imaginary* (Univ. of Michigan Press, 2011), 22.

Chantal Mouffe, *Agonistics: Thinking the World Politically* (Verso, 2013), 9.

Wallace Stevens, *The Necessary Angel: Essays on Reality and the Imagination* (Vintage, 1965), 13, 20.

Kim Addonizio, Interview by Tod Marshall, *Range of the Possible: Conversations with Contemporary Poets*, ed. Tod Marshall (Eastern Washington Univ. Press, 2002), 5.

Meena Alexander, "What Use Is Poetry?," *World Literature Today* 87.5 (2013): 19.

Kazim Ali, "An Interview with Kazim Ali," in *Our Deep Gossip: Conversations with Gay Writers on Poetry and Desire*, ed. Christopher Hennessy (Univ. of Wisconsin Press, 2013), 238.

Derek Attridge, "Contemporary Afrikaans Fiction and English Translation: Singularity and the Question of Minor Languages," *Singularity and Transnational Poetics*, ed. Birgit Mara Kaiser (Routledge, 2015), 66.

Mary Jo Bang, "Poetics Statement," in *Eleven More American Women Poets in the 21st Century: Poetics across North America*, ed. Claudia Rankine and Lisa Sewell (Wesleyan Univ. Press, 2012), 30–31.

Dan Beachy-Quick, *A Brighter Word Than Bright: Keats at Work* (Univ. of Iowa Press, 2013), 16.

Robin Becker, Untitled comment on "Dreaming at the Rexall Drug," in *What Will Suffice: Contemporary American Poets on the Art of Poetry*, ed. Christopher Buckley and Christopher Merrill (Gibbs Smith, 1995), 5.

Rosebud Ben-Oni, "Profiles in Poetics: Rosebud Ben-Oni," *Womens Quarterly Conversation* (11 November 2013). http://womensquarterlyconversation.com/category/rosebud-ben-oni/

Charles Bernstein, *Content's Dream: Essays 1975–1984* (Sun & Moon Press, 1986), 286.

Reginald Dwayne Betts, "An Abridged Version," *The Racial Imaginary: Writers on Race in the Life of the Mind*, ed. Claudia Rankine, Beth Loffreda, and Max King Cap (Fence Books, 2015), 236.

Tamiko Beyer, "Notes towards a queer::eco::poetics," Doveglion Press (29 November 2010). http://www.doveglion.com/2010/11/notes-towards-a-queerecopoetics-by-tamiko-beyer/

Frank Bidart, "An Interview—With Mark Halliday," in *In the Western Night: Collected Poems 1965–90* (Farrar Straus Giroux, 1990), 241.

Darren Bifford, "Metaphor and Ecological Responsibility," in *Lyric Ecology: An Appreciation of the Work of Jan Zwicky*, ed.

Mark Dickinson and Clare Goulet (Cormorant Books, 2010), 194.

Remica L. Bingham, "Blessed Condemnation: Interconnection and Reverence in *Black Nature,*" *Callaloo* 34:3 (Summer 2011): 771.

Sven Birkerts, *Readings* (Graywolf Press, 1999), 68.

Walid Bitar, "Flash Interview #1: Walid Bitar," *The Véhicule Press Blog* (4 December 2008). http://vehiculepress.blogspot.com/2008/12/flash-interview-with-walid-bitar.html

Sheila Black, "Waiting to Be Dangerous: Disability and Confessionalism," *Beauty is a Verb: The New Poetry of Disability*, ed. Jennifer Bartlett, Sheila Black, and Micheal Northen (Cincos Puntos Press, 2011), 206.

Jaswinder Bolina, "Writing Like a White Guy," *A Sense of Regard: Essays on Poetry and Race*, ed. Laura McCullough (Univ. of Georgia Press, 2015), 172.

Roo Borson, "Poetry as Knowing," in *Poetry and Knowing: Speculative Essays & Interviews*, ed. Tim Lilburn (Quarry Press, 1995), 124.

Amaranth Borsuk, "Interview with Amaranth Borsuk," in Andy Fitch, *Sixty Morning Talks* (Ugly Duckling Presse, 2014), 17.

David Borthwick, "Introduction," *Entanglements: New Ecopoetry*, ed. David Knowles and Sharon Blackie (Two Ravens Press, 2012), xx.

Marianne Boruch, *Poetry's Old Air* (Univ. of Michigan Press, 1995), 5.

Adam Bradley, *Book of Rhymes: The Poetics of Hip Hop* (BasicCivitas, 2009), 5.

Andrea Brady, "Tom Raworth: Poetry and Public Pleasure," in *Poetry and Public Language*, ed. Tony Lopez and Anthony Caleshu (Shearsman Books, 2007), 26.

Philip Brady, *By Heart: Reflections of a Rust Belt Bard* (Univ. of Tennessee Press, 2008), ix–x.

Stephanie Brown, "Not a Perfect Mother," *The Grand Permission: New Writings on Poetics and Motherhood*, ed. Patricia Dienstfrey and Brenda Hillman (Wesleyan Univ. Press, 2003), 31.

Stephen Burt, *Close Calls with Nonsense: Reading New Poetry* (Graywolf Press, 2009), xi.

David Caplan, *Questions of Possibility: Contemporary Poetry and Poetic Form* (Oxford Univ. Press, 2005), 11, 14.

Kristen *Case, American Pragmatism and Poetic Practice: Crosscurrents from Emerson to Susan Howe* (Camden House, 2011), 16–17.

Kate Cayley, "BWS 07.05.14," an interview by Daniel Perry, Brockton Writers Series blog (16 April 2014). https://brocktonwritersseries.wordpress.com/2014/04/16/bws-07-05-14-kate-cayley/

Subarno Chattarji, *Memories of a Lost War: American Poetic Responses to the Vietnam War* (Oxford Univ. Press, 2001), 2–3, 225–6.

Lisa D. Chávez, "Not Metaphor but Magic: The 'How' and Why of Narrative Poetry," in *Mentor and Muse: Essays from Poets to Poets*, ed. Blas Falconer, Beth Martinelli, and Helena Mesa (Southern Illinois Univ. Press, 2010), 41.

Jan Conn, "An Interview with Jan Conn," conducted by Sharon Caseburg, *Contemporary Verse 2* 30:3 (2008), excerpted at http://www.contemporaryverse2.ca/en/interviews/excerpt/an-interview-with-jan-conn

Stuart Cooke, "Tracing a Trajectory from Songpoetry to Contemporary Aboriginal Poetry," *A Companion to Australian Aboriginal Literature*, ed. Belinda Wheeler (Camden House, 2013), 89, 92–3.

Adam Dickinson, "*12 or 20 questions*: with Adam Dickinson," 12 or 20 questions (1 October 2007). http://12or20questions.blogspot.ca/2007/10/12-or-20-questions-with-adam-dickinson.html

Michael Dowdy, *American Political Poetry in the 21st Century* (Palgrave Macmillan, 2007), 194.

Camille T. Dungy, *"Introduction"* to *Black Nature: Four Centuries of African American Nature Poetry* (Univ. of Georgia Press, 2009), xxviii.

Rachel Blau DuPlessis, *Blue Studios: Poetry and Its Cultural Work* (Univ. of Alabama Press, 2006), 101–2.

Craig Dworkin, *"Seja Marginal,"* *The Consequence of Innovation: 21st Century Poetics*, ed. Craig Dworkin (Roof Books, 2008), 13.

Clayton Eshleman, *Companion Spider: Essays* (Wesleyan Univ. Press, 2002), 25.

Sandra Maria Esteves, Interview in *A Poet's Truth: Conversations with Latino/Latina Poets*, ed. Bruce Allen Dick (Univ. of Arizona Press, 2003), 52.

Blas Falconer, "Falconer, Melendez, León, Murillo: A Latino Quartet," Poetry Society of America. http://www.poetrysociety.org/psa/poetry/crossroads/interviews/ALatinoQuartet/

Jonathan Farmer, "Beauty and Violence," *The Slate Book Review* (31 March 2012). http://www.slate.com/articles/arts/books/2012/03/paisley_rekdal_s_poetry_of_beauty_and_violence_.html

Michael Farrell, "Interview with Michael Farrell," *Poetry International* (1 July 2011). http://www.poetryinternationalweb.net/pi/site/cou_article/item/20530/Interview-with-Michael-Farrell/en

Gene Fendt, *Love Song for the Life of the Mind: An Essay on the Purpose of Comedy* (The Catholic University of America Press, 2007), 52.

Ann Fisher-Wirth, "A Scattering, a Shining," in *The Ecopoetry Anthology*, ed. Ann Fisher-Wirth and Laura-Gray Street (Trinity Univ. Press, 2013), xxxv.

Deborah Fleming, "Landscape and the Self in W. B. Yeats and Robinson Jeffers," *Ecopoetry: A Critical Introduction*, ed. J. Scott Bryson (Univ. of Utah Press, 2002), 43.

Kit Fryatt, "'Norms and Forms': 10 Years of the British & Irish Poets e-mail list," in *Poetry and Public Language*, ed. Tony Lopez and Anthony Caleshu (Shearsman Books, 2007), 92.

Forrest Gander, *A Faithful Existence: Reading, Memory, and Transcendence* (Shoemaker & Hoard, 2005), 43.

J. Neil C. Garcia, "Translation and the Problem of Realism in Philippine Literature in English," *Kritika Kultura* 23 (2014): 119–20.

Suzanne Gardinier, *A World That Will Hold All the People* (Univ. of Michigan Press, 1996), 2–3.

Ulrikka S. Gernes, "Poetry as a Language of Resistance," interview by paolo da costa, on paolo da costa personal blog (12 December 2000). http://www.paulodacosta.ca/poetry-as-a-language-of-resistance/

Ranjan Ghosh, "The Figure that Robert Frost's Poetics Make: Singularity and Sanskrit Poetic Theory," *Singularity and Transnational Poetics*, ed. Birgit Mara Kaiser (Routledge, 2015), 134.

Melissa Girard, "'Jeweled Bindings': Modernist Women's Poetry and the Limits of Sentimentality," *The Oxford Handbook of Modern and Contemporary Poetry*, ed. Cary Nelson (Oxford Univ. Press, 2012), 116.

Diane Glancy, *Claiming Breath* (Univ. of Nebraska Press, 1992), 83.

Veronica Golos, "The Blind Spot," in "Poetry and Race Roundtable," *Evening Will Come: A Monthly Journal of Poetics* 10 (October 2011). http://www.thevolta.org/ewc10-racer-oundtable-p13.html

Janice Gould, "Poems as Maps in American Indian Women's Writing," *Speak to Me Words: Essays on Contemporary American Indian Poetry*, ed. Dean Rader and Janice Gould (Univ. of Arizona Press, 2003), 22.

Piotr Gwiazda, "The Beleaguered Mind," in Grzegorz Wróblewski, *Kopenhaga*, trans. Piotr Gwiazda (Zephyr Press, 2013), ix.

Rachel Hadas, *Merrill, Cavafy, Poems, and Dreams* (Univ. of Michigan Press, 2000), 42.

Joseph Harrington, *Poetry and the Public: The Social Form of Modern US Poetics* (Wesleyan Univ. Press, 2002), 5.

Robert Hass, *What Light Can Do: Essays on Art, Imagination, and the Natural World* (Ecco, 2012), 78.

Travis Hedge Coke, "Identity Indictment," *A Sense of Regard: Essays on Poetry and Race*, ed. Laura McCullough (Univ. of Georgia Press, 2015), 117.

Brian Henderson, "New Syntaxes in McCaffery and Nichol: Emptiness, Transformation, Serenity," *Essays on Canadian Writing* 37 (Spring 1989), 1.

Jane Hilberry, "Father and Daughter Poets–Jane and Conrad Hilberry–3 Questions," interview by Miriam Sagan, at http://miriamswell.wordpress.com/2011/01/11/father-and-daughter-poets-jane-and-conrad-hilberry-3-questions/

Sean Hill, "What Spills Over and What Urges the Spill: Some Whys and Wherefores of *Dangerous Goods*," *Evening Will Come: A Monthly Journal of Poetics* 50 (February 2015). http://www.thevolta.org/ewc50-shill-p1.html

Brenda Hillman, "Twelve Writings toward a Poetics of Alchemy, Dread, Inconsistency, Betweenness, and California Geological Syntax," *American Women Poets in the 21ˢᵗ Century: Where Lyric Meets Language*, ed. Claudia Rankine and Juliana Spahr (Wesleyan Univ. Press, 2002), 277–8.

Cynthia Hogue, *Scheming Women: Poetry, Privilege, and the Politics of Subjectivity* (SUNY Press, 1995), 1–2.

Ailish Hopper, "The Gentle Art of Making Enemies," *A Sense of Regard: Essays on Poetry and Race*, ed. Laura McCullough (Univ. of Georgia Press, 2015), 183.

Ishion Hutchinson, "Ishion Hutchinson Interview," *Poetry International* (16 January 2012). https://pionline.wordpress.com/2012/01/16/1405/

Oren Izenberg, *Being Numerous: Poetry and the Ground of Social Life* (Princeton Univ. Press, 2011), 33.

Pierre Joris, *A Nomad Poetics: Essays* (Wesleyan Univ. Press, 2003), 112.

Bettina Judd, "Writing About Race," *The Racial Imaginary: Writers on Race in the Life of the Mind*, ed. Claudia Rankine, Beth Loffreda, and Max King Cap (Fence Books, 2015), 265.

Birgit Mara Kaiser, "*Singularity and Transnational Poetics*," Singularity and Transnational Poetics, ed. Birgit Mara Kaiser (Routledge, 2015), 12.

AnaLouise Keating, "(De)Centering the Margins?: Identity Politics and Tactical (Re)Naming," *Other Sisterhoods: Literary Theory and Women of Color*, ed. Sandra Kumamoto Stanley (Univ. of Illinois Press, 1998), 25–26.

Vandana Khanna, "The Stories in My Ears," *Others Will Enter the Gates: Immigrant Poets on Poetry, Influences, and Writing in America*, ed. Abayomi Animashaun (Black Lawrence Press, 2015), 230.

Robert Kocik, *Supple Science: A Robert Kocik Primer*, ed. Michael Cross and Thom Donovan (On Contemporary Practice, 2013), 214.

Jee Leong Koh, "Diary," personal blog (30 June 2015). http:// jeeleong.blogspot.com/

Yahia Lababidi, "Aphorisms," *AGNI Online* (2009). http://www. bu.edu/agni/essays/online/2009/lababidi.html

Ed Bok Lee, "Speaker in a Future Age: Ed Bok Lee on Poetry, Places and the Death of Tongues," interview by Sueyeun Juliette Lee, *The Margins* (28 November 2012). http://aaww. org/speaker-in-a-future-age-ed-bok-lee-on-poetry-places-and-the-death-of-tongues/

Gary Lenhart, *The Stamp of Class: Reflections on Poetry & Social Class* (Univ. of Michigan Press, 2006), 5, 112.

Mari L'Esperance, "Interview: What We Know About Mari L'Esperance," *jmww* (1 February 2010). https://jmwwblog.wordpress.com/2010/02/01/ interview-what-we-know-about-mari-lesperance/

Sandra Lim, "Open Letter," *The Racial Imaginary: Writers on Race in the Life of the Mind*, ed. Claudia Rankine, Beth Loffreda, and Max King Cap (Fence Books, 2015), 255.

James Longenbach, *The Resistance to Poetry* (Univ. of Chicago Press, 2004), 101.

Rupert Loydell, *Encouraging Signs: Interviews, Essays & Conversations* (Shearsman Books, 2013), 41.

Elizabeth Macklin, "'It's a Woman's Prerogative to Change Her Mind,'" *By Herself: Women Reclaim Poetry*, ed. Molly McQuade (Graywolf Press, 2000), 23.

Barbara Maloutas, "Her Not Blessed," *Les Figues* (18 May 2010). http://lesfigues.blogspot.com/2010/05/her-not-blessed-by-barbara-maloutas.html

Ajuan Maria Mance, *Inventing Black Women: African American Women Poets and Self-Representation, 1877–2000* (Univ. of Tennessee Press, 2007), 126.

Valerie Martínez, Interview by Carmelia Padilla, *El Palacio* (August 2010), 30. http://www.elpalacio.org/articles/interviews/martinezinterview.pdf

Farid Matuk, "From Circumstance to Constellation: Richard Pryor, Resistance, and the Racial Imaginary's Archive," *The Racial Imaginary: Writers on Race in the Life of the Mind*, ed. Claudia Rankine, Beth Loffreda, and Max King Cap (Fence Books, 2015), 143–44.

Sophie Mayer, "'Our Leaves of Paper Will Be / Dancing Lightly': Indigenous Poetics," *The Oxford Handbook of Indigenous American Literature*, ed. James H. Cox and Daniel Heath Justice (Oxford Univ. Press, 2014), 240.

Olivia McCannon, "'The Desire to Live More Intensely,'" *Modern Poetry in Translation* 1 (2013), 109.

Lynn Melnick, "Introduction" to "Poets' Roundtable on Person and Persona," by Metta Sáma, Alex Dimitrov, and Lynn Melnick, *Los Angeles Review of Books* (20 October 2013). http://lareviewofbooks.org/essay/poets-roundtable-on-person-and-persona

Douglas Messerli, "Making Things Difficult," an interview by

Charles Bernstein, *Jacket 2.* http://jacketmagazine.com/28/bern-iv-mess.html

Philip Metres, *Behind the Lines: War Resistance Poetry on the American Homefront Since 1941* (Univ. of Iowa Press, 2007), 233–34.

Aaron M. Moe, *Zoopoetics: Animals and the Making of Poetry* (Lexington Books, 2014), 27–28.

Sawnie Morris, "Review of *Each and Her* by Valerie Martínez," *Taos Journal of Poetry and Art.* http://www.taosjournalofpoetry.com/review-of-each-and-her-by-valerie-martinez/

Mihaela Moscaliuc, "Code Switching, Multilanguaging, and Language Alterity," *A Sense of Regard: Essays on Poetry and Race*, ed. Laura McCullough (Univ. of Georgia Press, 2015), 223.

Fred Moten, *In the Break: The Aesthetics of the Black Radical Tradition* (Univ. of Minnesota Press, 2003), 96.

Jennifer Moxley, "Fragments from a Broken Poetics," *Chicago Review* 55:2 (Spring 2010), 19.

Nathanaël, *Sisyphus, Outdone. Theatres of the Catastrophal* (Nightboat Books, 2012), 79.

Christopher Nealon, T*he Matter of Capital: Poetry and Crisis in the American Century* (Harvard Univ. Press, 2011), 7, 9.

Charu Nivedita, "Author's Parole," an interview by Tishani Doshi, personal website (28 January 2015). http://charunivedita.com/2015/01/28/authors-parole-interviewed-by-tishani-doshi/

Urayoán Noel, "Unstatement," personal website. http://urayoan-noel.com/

Alicia Suskin Ostriker, Dancing at the *Devil's Party: Essays on Poetry, Politics, and the Erotic* (Univ. of Michigan Press, 2000), 9.

Kristin Palm, "Open Letter," *The Racial Imaginary: Writers on Race in the Life of the Mind*, ed. Claudia Rankine, Beth Loffreda, and Max King Cap (Fence Books, 2015), 261.

Josephine Park, "Asian American Poetry," *The Oxford Handbook of Modern and Contemporary Poetry*, ed. Cary Nelson (Oxford Univ. Press, 2012), 405.

Edward M. Pavlić, *Crossroads Modernism: Descent and Emergence in African-American Literary Culture* (Univ. of Minnesota Press, 2002), xii.

Emmy Pérez, "Healing and the Poetic Line," *A Broken Thing: Poets on the Line*, ed. Emily Rosko and Anton Vander Zee (Univ. of Iowa Press, 2011), 184.

Katie Peterson, "The Suffering World: Poets Grieve," *The Boston Review* (1 January 2012). http://www.bostonreview.net/poetry/katie-peterson-carson-levin-schnackenberg

Jeffrey Pethybridge, "To Be The Imaginary (In April)," *NPM Daily*. http://npmdaily.tumblr.com/post/82165665453/jeffrey-pethybridge

Carl Phillips, *Coin of the Realm: Essays on the Life and Art of Poetry* (Graywolf Press, 2004), 92.

Rowan Ricardo Phillips, *When Blackness Rhymes with Blackness* (Dalkey Archive Press, 2010), 12.

Shabnam Piryaei, "To Be a Poet in America," *Others Will Enter the Gates: Immigrant Poets on Poetry, Influences, and Writing in America*, ed. Abayomi Animashaun (Black Lawrence Press, 2015), 180–81.

Vanessa Place, "Interview with Vanessa Place," by Jacob Bromberg, *The White Review* (October 2014). http://www.thewhitereview.org/interviews/interview-with-vanessa-place/

Kristin Prevallet, *I, Afterlife: Essay in Mourning Time* (Essay Press, 2007), 48.

Lia Purpura, *Rough Likeness* (Sarabande Books, 2011), 27.

Bernard W. Quetchenbach, *Back from the Far Field: American Nature Poetry in the Late Twentieth Century* (Univ. Press of Virginia, 2000), 147, 157.

Dean Rader, "Reading the Visual, Seeing the Verbal: Text and

Image in Recent American Indian Literature and Art," *The Oxford Handbook of Indigenous American Literature*, ed. James H. Cox and Daniel Heath Justice (Oxford Univ. Press, 2014), 300.

Howard Rambsy II, *The Black Arts Enterprise and the Production of African American Poetry* (Univ. of Michigan Press, 2011), 4.

Margaret Randall, "Piercing the Walls," in *Cross Worlds: Transcultural Poetics: An Anthology*, ed. Anne Waldman and Laura Wright (Coffee House Press, 2014), 277.

John Redmond, "Auden in Ireland," *The Oxford Handbook of Contemporary British and Irish Poetry*, ed. Peter Robinson (Oxford Univ. Press, 2013), 425.

Peter Robinson, "Introduction: The Limits and Openness of the Contemporary," *The Oxford Handbook of Contemporary British and Irish Poetry*, ed. Peter Robinson (Oxford Univ. Press, 2013), 4–5.

Lee Ann Roripaugh, "Poem as Mirror Box: Mirror Neurons, Emotions, Phantom Limbs, and Poems of Loss and Elegy," *jubilat* 21 (Spring 2012), 107.

Mary Ruefle, *Madness, Rack, and Honey: Collected Lectures* (Wave Books, 2012), 131.

Metta Sáma, "'Imagination! Who Can Sing Thy Force?' (—Phillis Wheatley)," in "Poets' Roundtable on Person and Persona," by Metta Sáma, Alex Dimitrov, and Lynn Melnick, *Los Angeles Review of Books* (20 October 2013). http://lareviewofbooks. org/essay/poets-roundtable-on-person-and-persona

Mary Ann Samyn, "Bring Yourself Along," in *Mentor and Muse: Essays from Poets to Poets*, ed. Blas Falconer, Beth Martinelli, and Helena Mesa (Southern Illinois Univ. Press, 2010), 222.

Jane Satterfield, "'Lucifer Matches': Epistles and Other Conversations (The Epistolary Lyric)," in *Mentor and Muse: Essays from Poets to Poets*, ed. Blas Falconer, Beth Martinelli, and Helena Mesa (Southern Illinois Univ. Press, 2010), 189.

Zach Savich, "Eleven Essays I'm Not Writing About

Contemporary Poetry," *The Philadelphia Review of Books* (2 September 2013). http://philareview.com/2013/09/02/eleven-essays-im-not-writing-about-contemporary-poetry/

Mara Scanlon, "Introduction: Hearing Over," *Poetry and Dialogism: Hearing Over*, ed. Mara Scanlon and Chad Engbers (Palgrave Macmillan, 2014), 3.

James Scully, *Line Break: Poetry as Social Practice* (Curbstone Press, 2004), 145.

James Scully, "Poetry: Up Against the Wall of the 11ᵗʰ Thesis," Talk delivered at the Radical Philosophy Association 8ᵗʰ Biennial Conference, SF State University, 28 Oct. 2008. A few comments [bracketed] have been added.

Robert Sheppard, "Public Poetics: The Manifesto of the Poetry Society (1976)," in *Poetry and Public Language*, ed. Tony Lopez and Anthony Caleshu (Shearsman Books, 2007), 231–2.

Anis Shivani, Interview by Loren Kleinman, "Polemic, Prose Writer, Poet & Chef: An In-depth Interview With Anis Shivani," *Huffington Post* (13 February 2014). http://www.huffingtonpost.com/loren-kleinman/polemic-prose-writer-poet_b_4783170.html

Anne Simpson, "Look at Things Like This," in *Lyric Ecology: An Appreciation of the Work of Jan Zwicky*, ed. Mark Dickinson and Clare Goulet (Cormorant Books, 2010), 155.

Andrea Witzke Slot, "Dialogic Poetry as Emancipatory Technology: Ventriloquy and Voiceovers in the Rhythmic Junctures of Harryette Mullen's *Muse & Drudge*," *Poetry and Dialogism: Hearing Over*, ed. Mara Scanlon and Chad Engbers (Palgrave Macmillan, 2014), 161.

Cherry Smyth, "Queer Poetry by Definition," *Poetry Review* 102:4 (Winter 2012).

Timothy Steele, *Missing Measures: Modern Poetry and the Revolt Against Meter* (The Univ. of Arkansas Press, 1990), 294.

Lisa M. Steinman, "'So As to Be One Having Some Way of Being One Having Some Way of Working': Marianne Moore and Literary Tradition," *Gendered Modernisms: American Women Poets and Their Readers*, ed. Margaret Dickie and Thomas Travisano (Univ. of Pennsylvania Press, 1996), 97.

Robert Stewart, *Outside Language: Essays* (Helicon Nine Editions, 2003), 41.

Laura-Gray Street, "The Roots of It," in *The Ecopoetry Anthology*, ed. Ann Fisher-Wirth and Laura-Gray Street (Trinity Univ. Press, 2013), xxxviii.

James D. Sullivan, "Reading the Process: Stuart Hall, TV News, Heteroglossia, and Poetry," *Poetry and Dialogism: Hearing Over*, ed. Mara Scanlon and Chad Engbers (Palgrave Macmillan, 2014), 140–41.

Margo Tamez, "Conspiring with Margo Tamez," an interview by Lisa Alvarado, *Banderas News* (April 2007). http://www.banderasnews.com/0704/entbk-raveneye.htm

Jeffrey Wainwright, "'Space Available': A Poet's Decisions," *The Oxford Handbook of Contemporary British and Irish Poetry*, ed. Peter Robinson (Oxford Univ. Press, 2013), 228.

Joni Wallace, "Why Joni Wallace Reads (and Writes) Poetry," BookPeople's Blog (11 April 2011). https://bookpeopleblog.wordpress.com/2011/04/11/why-joni-wallace-reads-and-writes-poetry/

Jerry W. Ward, Jr., "Illocutionary Dimensions of Poetry: Lee's 'A Poem to Complement Other Poems,'" *The Furious Flowering of African American Poetry*, ed. Joanne V. Gabbin (Univ. Press of Virginia, 1999), 138.

Michael Waters, "Writing by Ear: An Interview with Michael Waters," in Tony Leuzzi, *Passwords Primeval: 20 American Poets in Their Own Words* (BOA Editions, 2012), 23.

Afaa Michael Weaver, "My Walking Shoes: Working-Class Origins of an American Lyric," Poetry Foundation (14 May 2013). http://www.poetryfoundation.org/article/245930

Jonathan Weinert, "This Nothing This Heaven: Notes on W. S. Merwin's *The Shadow of Sirius.*" *The Cresset* (2012). http://

thecresset.org/2012/Trinity/Weinert_T2012.html

Lesley Wheeler, *The Poetics of Enclosure: American Women Poets from Dickinson to Dove* (Univ. of Tennessee Press, 2002), 6.

Susan Wheeler, "Poetry, Mattering?," *By Herself: Women Reclaim Poetry*, ed. Molly McQuade (Graywolf Press, 2000), 324.

Phillip B. Williams, "'Severed Hands Comb the Air': An Interview with Phillip B. Williams," *The Collagist* (11 January 2015). http://thecollagist.com/collagist-blog/2015/1/11/severed-hands-comb-the-air-an-interview-with-phillip-b-willi.html

Eleanor Wilner, "Playing the Changes," *By Herself: Women Reclaim Poetry*, ed. Molly McQuade (Graywolf Press, 2000), 227.

Christian Wiman, *Ambition and Survival: Becoming a Poet* (Copper Canyon Press, 2007), 112.

Shira Wolosky, *Poetry and Public Discourse in Nineteenth-Century America* (Palgrave Macmillan, 2010), 3.

Paul Woodruff, *The Ajax Dilemma: Justice, Fairness, and Rewards* (Oxford Univ. Press, 2011), 180, n. 183–4.

C. D. Wright, *Cooling Time: An American Poetry Vigil* (Copper Canyon Press, 2005), 59.

Changming Yuan, "Die in Poetry, or Live Forever," *Evening Will Come: A Monthly Journal of Poetics* 48 (December 2014). http://www.thevolta.org/ewc48-cyuan-p1.html

Poetries: Robert Bringhurst, *The Tree of Meaning: Language, Mind and Ecology* (Counterpoint, 2008), 41.

Left: Emmanuel Levinas, *Otherwise Than Being or Beyond Essence*, trans. Alphonso Lingis (Duquesne Univ. Press, 1998), 12.

Citizens: Amartya Sen, *Rationality and Freedom* (Harvard Univ. Press, 2002), 546.

Ego: Laura (Riding) Jackson, *Though Gently* (The Seizin Press, 1930, as reprinted in Delmar 8 (Winter 2002)), 19.

Necessity: Karl Marx, *Selected Writings*, ed. David McLellan (Oxford Univ. Press, 1977), 197.

Self : World: Judith Butler, *Giving an Account of Oneself* (Fordham Univ. Press, 2005), 28.

Making: Robert Pogue Harrison, *The Dominion of the Dead* (Univ. of Chicago Press, 2003), 17.

Listen: Gerald L. Bruns, *The Material of Poetry: Sketches for a Philosophical Poetics* (Univ. of Georgia Press, 2005), 43.

Convergence: Herakleitos, trans. H. L. Hix, *The Yale Review* 103:2 (April 2015): 11.

Particularity: Donald Barthelme, *Not Knowing: The Essays and Interviews of Donald Barthelme*, ed. Kim Herzinger (Random House, 1997), 21.

Between: John Rajchman, *Constructions* (MIT Press, 1998), 15.

Interconnection: Rosi Braidotti, *Transpositions: On Nomadic Ethics* (Polity, 2006), 35.

Prayer: Simone Weil, *Gravity and Grace*, trans. Arthur Wills (Univ. of Nebraska Press, 1997), 66.

Different: Peter Sloterdijk, *You Must Change Your Life*, trans. Wieland Hoban (Polity, 2013), 25–26.

Time: Augustine, *The Confessions of St. Augustine*, trans. Rex Warner (New American Library, 1963), 282.

Information: Walter Benjamin, *The Arcades Project*, trans. Howard Eiland and Kevin McLaughlin (Harvard Univ. Press, 1999), 804.

Nuance: Louis Zukofsky, *Prepositions: The Collected Critical Essays* (Univ. of California Press, 1981), 7.

Attention: Iris Murdoch, *The Sovereignty of Good* (Ark, 1985), 67.

Inexplicable: Louise Glück, *Proofs and Theories: Essays on Poetry* (Ecco, 1994), 45.

Memory: Ngũgĩ wa Thiong'o, *Something Torn and New: An African Renaissance* (BasicCivitas Books, 2009), 112, 114.

Reimagine: Hans-Georg Gadamer, *The Relevance of the Beautiful and Other Essays*, trans. Nicholas Walker, ed. Robert Bernasconi (Cambridge Univ. Press, 1986), 91.

Refusal: Sara Ahmed, *The Promise of Happiness* (Duke Univ. Press, 2010), 68–69.

Form: G. W. Leibniz, *Philosophical Essays*, trans. Roger Ariew and Daniel Garber (Hackett, 1989), 168.